SHARON WHITELEY AND ANN MARIE CHIASSON MD

BARE OOT
W SDOM

REDFeather

Better Health through
GROUNDING

Designed by Danielle D. Farmer
Cover design by Justin Watkinson

Type set in Helvetica Neue LT Pro / Sabon LT Std

ISBN: 978-0-7643-5544-8
Printed in China

Published by Red Feather Mind, Body, Spirit
An imprint of Schiffer Publishing, Ltd.
4880 Lower Valley Road
Atglen, PA 19310
Phone: (610) 593-1777; Fax: (610) 593-2002
E-mail: Info@schifferbooks.com
Web: www.redfeatherpub.com

For our complete selection of fine books on this and related subjects, please visit our website at www.schifferbooks.com. You may also write for a free catalog.

Schiffer Publishing's titles are available at special discounts for bulk purchases for sales promotions or premiums. Special editions, including personalized covers, corporate imprints, and excerpts, can be created in large quantities for special needs. For more information, contact the publisher.

We are always looking for people to write books on new and related subjects. If you have an idea for a book, please contact us at proposals@schifferbooks.com.

Other Schiffer Books on Related Subjects:

GET POSITIVE LIVE POSITIVE

Clearing the Negativity from Your Life

Melinda D. Carver

ISBN: 978-0-7643-5291-1

LIVING A LIFE IN BALANCE

An Elemental Journey of Self-Discovery

Cael SpiritHawk

ISBN: 978-0-7643-4748-1

It was approximately fifteen years ago while attending an American College of Cardiology meeting that I first met Clint Ober. In the manner of an hour this Earthing researcher introduced me to the science of grounding—and it forever changed my life! In fact, as a practicing integrative and invasive cardiologist with over four decades of experience, I can truthfully say that the two greatest "discoveries" during my professional lifetime have been learning about the discovery of Co Enzyme Q10 in 1982 and later the positive health impact that grounding has on our own body. Both are potential electron donors that enhance the generation of cellular energy via the production of adesosine triphosphate (ATP).

ATP is vital for heart health, as well as the energy of life itself. Whenever we can augment the production of ATP in the body at the cellular level we support vitality, creativity, and well-being, which reflect the vibration of our entire being. Indeed, vibration is the key to health and healing for every living thing. One of the easiest ways to enhance/increase/promote vibration is to put your bare feet in contact with the ground; walking on grounded footwear, and sleeping tethered to the Schumann energy of the earth.

In *Barefoot Wisdom* Sharon Whiteley and her co-author, Ann Marie Chaisson MD, explain in very simple terms the essence of the Schumann energy—the Mother Earth energy field of 7.83 HZ—and offer proven, scientific methods that will help heal your life. Many of you will grasp the insights readily, but others will need repetition of new concepts involving the science behind the earth's energy field and the simplicity of connecting to that energy to promote healing and balance.

Some of us need repetition and reinforcement to help integrate new information and debunk the many rigid beliefs systems we harbor. In other words, repetition of scientific data will help to alter our preconceived beliefs about health and healing, and bring us around to the true meaning of Mother Earth energy.

Barefoot Wisdom is chocked full of real-life experiences and remarkable individual case studies. I loved reading this book and feel that the knowledge gleaned will be instrumental for the reader to optimize his or her own health. In living a higher vibrational lifestyle that I recommend to my own readers, grounding is one of six basic elements that we all need to include in our daily life. This book will get you started on your journey in embracing such a simple, remarkable and often overlooked component to optimal health. Trust me, Nature heals, and grounding is the most basic and primitive way to get your life back!

Stephen T. Sinatra MD, FACC, CBT, CNS
Co-author: *Earthing: the Greatest Health Discovery Ever!*
Author: *Optimum Health: A Natural Lifesaving Prescription for Your Body and Mind*

TO PLANET
EARTH

CONTENTS

6 — ACKNOWLEDGMENTS

7 — PREFACE:
Our Grounding Story

12 — CHAPTER ONE:
Step into Better Health

18 — CHAPTER TWO:
What the Natives Knew

24 — CHAPTER THREE:
Earth Science 101 and Your Health

30 — CHAPTER FOUR:
Healthy Connections

36 — CHAPTER FIVE:
Change Your Life Naturally

42 — CHAPTER SIX:
Expert Connections

49 — CHAPTER SEVEN:
The Myths, Misconceptions, and
Downright Skeptics

55 — CHAPTER EIGHT:
What Grounding Means

61 — CHAPTER NINE:
Barefoot Wisdom from A to Z

75 — CHAPTER TEN:
How to Get and Stay Grounded Wherever
You Are

83 — CHAPTER ELEVEN:
Energy Medicine: The Earth as Treatment
Table

86 — CHAPTER TWELVE:
Getting Your Hands . . . and Feet . . .
around Your Health

90 — CHAPTER THIRTEEN:
Mother Nature and Earth Mothers

95 — CHAPTER FOURTEEN:
Feet on the Ground

99 — CHAPTER FIFTEEN:
Ancient Movement Arts and Grounding

104 — CHAPTER SIXTEEN:
Take a Walk on the Wild Side

108 — CHAPTER SEVENTEEN:
Walking into the Future: Prescription
"Vitamin Ground"

114 — ENDNOTES

117 — BIBLIOGRAPHY

118 — INDEX

Better Health through
GROUNDING

ACKNOWLEDGMENTS

Books don't write themselves. Whether they're inspired by fact or fiction, authors like us have help, often unseen, along every step of the journey. If not for the work of grounding pioneers Clinton Ober, Dr. Stephen Sinatra, and biophysicist Jim Oschman, and researchers Gaétan Chevalier and Melinda Connor, we would not have known about this abundant natural healing resource, let alone believed in it so much that we would write a book about it. Their research and findings prompted us to share with others who would benefit. We are indebted to them for teaching us—and now you—the benefits of getting grounded.

As we set out to write more about the history and practice of grounding through the ages, we interviewed amazing practitioners. They include Dr. Lewis Mehl-Madrona, whose insights on Native American culture enhanced our understanding of our relationship with Mother Nature; Howard Straus, author and VoiceAmerica personality, who generously shared his own personal grounding stories with us; natural health and intuitive physician Dr. Laura Koniver, who was incredibly generous with her personal journey into grounding and her medical perspective; and Judy Brooks, PBS radio show host and cocreator of her resource-rich *Healing Quest* program. We sought out shamanic healer Linda Hogan for her sage advice on Earthly energy and Emil De Toffol about man-made electromagnetic frequencies. We are grateful for their shared beliefs in natural healing.

We interviewed body, mind, spirit practitioners, including author and yogi Amy Weintraub, sleep specialist Dr. Rubin Naiman, and best-selling author and creative thinker Michael Gelb, who mindfully practices grounding every day no matter where he is in the world. We heard from athletes and motivational speakers, including Gold Medalist Adam Kreek and performance trainer Bob Babinski, who incorporate grounding exercises into their work. And we spoke with eternal optimist Jurriaan Kamp about natural healing solutions and the eminent Dr. Shamini Jain about the future of biofield medicine. A special thank you to each of them for their in-depth conversations and the precious time they spent speaking with us.

Filmmaker Steve Kroschel whole-heartedly shared about his walks into the wilderness, his grounding work with animals, and his documentaries. Philosophers, poets, and physicians from Aristotle to Wordsworth motivated us with their time-tested wisdom and timeless quotations. In addition, health luminaries and thought leaders whose books and articles we embraced added further insight. There are many others unnamed here who shared and showed us what grounding means to them. We thank them all for their connections and priceless contributions to this book.

Finally, our deepest appreciation goes out to our remarkable literary agent Cindy Clarke for her unwavering encouragement and belief in us. We are also honored that our publisher and editors saw the wisdom in our stories and our words. We hope that you will follow in our health-oriented footsteps.

With Gratitude,
Sharon Whiteley and Ann Marie Chiasson

NOW I SEE THE SECRET OF THE MAKING OF THE
BEST PERSONS. IT IS TO GROW IN THE OPEN AIR,
AND TO EAT AND SLEEP WITH THE EARTH.

—*Walt Whitman*

Our Grounding
STORY

SHARON WHITELEY
TAKES THE FIRST STEP

I was innocently sitting in a morning lecture at a health and wellness conference I attended at the last minute with a friend, in the fall of 2011 in Las Vegas of all places. Smoke filtered through the hallways and the *ka-ching* of slot machines echoed all around; hardly the venue I was expecting for this event. It was very early and my morning coffee hadn't yet seeped into my veins. But here I was, trying my best to be attentive. And it was here that I had my *aha!* moment about grounding.

I had been engaged in health and wellness for a number of years, personally and professionally, proactively keeping up-to-date on innovative technologies and treatments that could enhance and positively impact people's lives. While all of the information I garnered through many conferences, endless reading, and sought-after conversations with experts on traditional and alternative healing modalities was fascinating, what intrigued me most was learning about the connection between compromised health and our separation from nature. Recent studies revealed that as the world became more westernized and virtually doubled our life expectancies, it also created alarming disparities between ancient and present ways of living. Time tested ones. Modernization certainly introduced more creature comforts in our lives, but it also paved the way for the emergence of new diseases that are now thought to be rooted in a common cause: nature deficiency.

The more I discovered about nature deficiency in our modern, largely urbanized society, the more aware I became of its harmful effect on our bodies. It wasn't until I attended this conference, however, that I was introduced to a remedy that is there for the taking—and a free one at that. It was called grounding, also known as Earthing. I had never heard of the word "Earthing," or grounding as it related to health benefits. I thought it was something you did to kids when they blew curfew or misbehaved. Simply stated, grounding means tapping into the Earth's always accessible, powerful natural energy to rebalance our bodies and reclaim our health.

Grounding is not about faith healing or spiritual healing or what some might call woo-woo, crunchy granola. It certainly is not a snake oil remedy. And, you don't have to "believe" in it for it to work. It has nothing to do with "sending" energy. Nor is it a "technique." Rather, it's about reconnecting directly with something that's been around since the beginning of time—the Earth—and the natural energy-electrons, stored within it.

At this conference, I was riveted by extensive scientific findings documented by pioneers like Clint Ober, Dr. Stephen Sinatra, a cardiologist, and Martin Zucker, a health aficionado—authors of *Earthing: The Most Important Health Discovery Ever!* and also James Oschman, PhD, a leading-edge and highly respected biophysicist who stated, "Grounding and Earthing is as important for our health as sunshine and good nutrition." He punctuated this point by enthusiastically proclaiming in a documentary film called *GROUNDED*, "Grounding is as important as the discovery of penicillin." Their findings all pointed unequivocally to the positive health benefits of being more closely connected to the benefits bestowed on us from the Earth.

As I soon thereafter discovered, there is a great deal of substantiating scientific research behind the beneficial effects of grounding and its natural energy in the form of electrons they deliver back to us. Many studies show that becoming more electron-nourished also helps to neutralize the harmful free radicals found in modern-day bodies and aids in healing from the inside out. Reduction of inflammation, an insidious culprit causing many conditions and now further associated with numerous chronic diseases, is a major documented benefit.

Later that day at the conference while walking through the vendor-packed trade show aisles promising remedies—from supplements galore, stem cell treatments, and body enhancing implants—I couldn't stop from thinking about ways we could put everybody in the mainstream in touch with the benefits of getting grounded. I got that invisible "tap on the shoulder, stirred in the gut feeling" and halted in my tracks. That's when the ideas came to create specially designed products—specifically, conductive footwear that would ground you even on concrete city sidewalks and an easy-to-read book that credibly and in digestible lay terms, relayed the steps that people could utilize daily to dramatically improve their health.

I was living part time in Tucson at the time and during a stop there, after leaving the city of bright lights, I called my friend and coauthor, Ann Marie Chiasson, MD, to tell her about my exciting discovery. Ann Marie, a traditional medical doctor practicing and teaching integrative medicine, an author, and also a renowned expert on energy healing. A modern-day shaman if there ever was one. I asked for her take on grounding. Was it everything the studies claimed? Was it true that grounding could help us reclaim our health as the scientific research had indicated?

She looked at me head on but I could sense her eyes were rolling back in their sockets and she said, "Of course it's true. And it's a large part of what healed me from thirty years of chronic pain." She added, "I know someone you should meet here in town, Melinda Connor, a Ph.D. and esteemed researcher in the field of energy medicine." Lucky for me Melinda was in town and made time to get together. As emphatically, she shared her affirming views about the benefits of grounding and said as did Ann Marie, "I know someone you should meet."

She was talking about Jim Oschman, PhD, one of the field's best-known authorities on grounding. She put me in touch with Jim, and I immediately flew out to his home in New Hampshire, in a snowstorm no less, for the chance to speak with him face to face. I couldn't wait a minute longer. He, along with his wife, Nora, who often collaborates in his scientific research, confirmed that grounding was one of—if not the most important—health discoveries of our time.

I spent the next year doing my own research and connecting with scientists and the pioneers in the field of grounding. I also found out that many body and medical practitioners, high profile celebrities, and athletes already embraced grounding. But it hadn't become mainstream yet. I began to incorporate grounding into my everyday activities to access for myself nature's restorative energy. It was and remains life changing.

The concept of nature as healer is not new. Poets, scientists, and philosophers have long professed its power to nourish body, mind, and soul. In fact, nature has been our greatest health resource since the beginning of time. For thousands of years, mankind thrived by adapting and taking full advantage of the Earth's natural environments. But in the last few hundred years, as we moved in droves to urbanized areas, we have seen a mass human disengagement from nature. We live in a modern society today that, by its very essence, insulates us from the outside. We drive, fly, or take a train almost everywhere. We wear "new and improved" synthetic clothing and insulating footwear edging out cottons, leathers, and silks made from natural materials. In the summer, we head for air-conditioned cool. In inclement weather we don rubber-soled shoes and boots so as not to get our feet wet. Streets bury the ground we should be walking on. Asphalt turns parkland into concrete playgrounds. Raised in cities, many kids don't have the opportunity to run barefoot outside in the dirt and grass or swim in lakes, ponds, and salt rich oceans. Never before in history have people spent so little time in direct physical contact with the Earth. The consequences have not only pointed to a loss of vitality and health, but have indicated an increase in a number of noncommunicable diseases.

ANN MARIE CHIASSON
WALKS THE TALK, TOO

The simple act of grounding gives us a way to get back in touch with nature and its healing energy no matter where we live or work. I wondered that if I hadn't known about it before I attended that eye-opening conference, how many others weren't familiar with grounding? And so the idea for this book was born. Ann Marie shared this same vision and we were compelled to get this information out in the world in a way that would be meaningful, beneficial, and understandable to anyone who reads it. Dare we say, obvious? It's nature after all, and it's natural.

Take a read inside the book and you'll find barefoot wisdom rooted in the ages. Indigenous peoples were in touch with the life-giving energies of planet Earth 24/7, and that, scientists say, made all the difference. The Earth has always been the treatment table of choice, a place where healing energy was abundant, naturally sustainable, and free. After all, the function of the Earth is to support life. Our lives, urbanized, anesthetized, and sanitized, have followed right along. In our haste to reach the stars, we have forgotten about the treasure trove of riches that lay at our feet. The challenge—and the opportunity—is to integrate its energy back into our lifestyles today.

Taking the first step to better health is as easy as taking a walk outside. It's the best way we know to stay grounded in all that is naturally good for you. What's old is new again; being lauded, promoted, and celebrated today. The ancients were wise; they knew, and we promise you'll be able to easily put yourself into this picture.

CHAPTER ONE

THE EARTH HAS MUSIC FOR THOSE
WHO LISTEN.

—*William Shakespeare*

Step into Better
HEALTH

Mother Earth—life giving, life changing, the lifeblood of all living things—has gotten short shrift of late. Ever-evolving man-made technology is trumping a network of highly evolved earthly connections, as sprawling urban jungles are paving over landscapes that are naturally nurturing. But what's underfoot and overlooked as we walk into the future with a host of chronic ailments and disease-causing inflammation that may ultimately be our undoing is a naturally sustaining healing resource that's limitless, easy to access, scientifically documented—and free. It's called grounding, also known as Earthing.

GET
GROUNDED

The expression has been around for years. A colloquial phrase for getting real, being grounded means coming back down to Earth, getting centered, and reconnecting with what's really important in life. For those of us who associate being grounded with house arrest for blowing off curfew or breaking another parental rule while we were pushing our youthful boundaries, change your perspective and focus on the benefits you received when you were forced to take a time-out and think about things.

Maybe it wasn't a punishment after all. When you are grounded, you are aware of what's happening in the moment. You can breathe easier, feel calmness, and recharge effortlessly. You de-stress and detox, focus, and find clarity. You can touch and be in touch with your feelings, your surroundings, and yourself. Get grounded and you're on your way to restoring, replenishing, and revitalizing your health, mentally, physically, emotionally, and endlessly. You've heard the saying, "The best things in life are free." When it comes to grounding, we couldn't agree more.

All of this begs the question: In today's automated, increasingly virtual world, how do you make grounded connections that support human sustainability and better health?

AN EARLY MORNING WALK IS A BLESSING FOR THE WHOLE DAY.
—*Henry David Thoreau*

Grounding is as simple as taking a stroll outside on the grass, along a dirt path, or on a sandy beach. Barefoot is best, of course. There's an awareness to barefoot walking that feels light, free, and downright joyful. It feels good, and it's also good for you. If you have to wear shoes, which most of us do in our daily lives, put on a pair that have conductive or pure leather soles, and you'll get grounded.

It's not just about barefooting, however, which can also have its perils. Grounding also happens when you go for a swim in the ocean, take a dip in a lake, or wade in a stream. It happens when you lie down in dew-dampened grass, dig in a garden, plant flowers, do yard work, practice yoga alfresco, meditate in a meadow, sit on a rock, sunbathe, take a shower or a bath in running water, get a pedicure, and yes, even hug a tree—or at least perch up against one while reading, texting, or listening to your favorite tunes. In fact, any outdoor activity that puts you into direct contact with the Earth for a period of time will do; twenty to thirty minutes a day is all it takes, and of course, the more the better. All these allow for the transfer of electrons, from the Earth to your body, to occur. By increasing the number of electrons in your body, you naturally become more energized. You sleep better, you are less stressed, and your health improves. There's not one right way to get grounded; there are many. Earth to you can work wonders.

COME FORTH INTO THE LIGHT OF THINGS;
LET NATURE BE YOUR TEACHER.
—*William Wordsworth*

Extensive research explains why this happens. The Earth is a natural source of electrons and subtle electrical fields, energy that all living things use to live. We know that life itself, when you boil it down, is a flow of electrons. Every life-form has an innate need for them. Electrons are essential for the proper functioning of the immune, circulatory, and nervous systems, and are also needed for the synchronization of biorhythms and other physiological processes that allow humans to live healthful lives. Similarly, our bodies are electrical systems. Throughout our evolutionary history, our internal electrical homeostasis has been maintained and regulated by direct bodily contact with the Earth.

Simply put, your immune system functions optimally when your body has an adequate supply of the Earth's natural energy. When you touch the ground without interference, your body naturally absorbs its electrons. While any body part will do, you'll get the bigger boost through the soles of your feet. With more than 7,000 nerve endings in each foot, it's no surprise that walking grounded is the best way to recharge your health, effortlessly.

WHEN FREE
ISN'T A GOOD THING

We're talking about free radicals. Ever present in our modern lifestyles, free radicals—scavenger molecules that are missing an electron—cause cell mutations, damage immune function, exacerbate wrinkles and aging, and are a contributing cause behind many chronic diseases including cancer, heart disease, arthritis, Alzheimer's disease, Parkinson's disease, and vision loss. Disease tends to create free radicals, as do environmental pollution and poor nutrition, unfortunate by-products of life today. Disturbingly, our own bodies are creating these opportunistic atoms at an astonishing speed.

The antidote to free radicals is the antioxidant. We make some antioxidants naturally and others are traditionally supplied in our diets by eating fruits and vegetables. Everyday environmental influences, among them stress, poor eating habits, and pollution, have increased our need for antioxidants well beyond what our bodies are capable of producing on their own, certainly beyond what we eat.

Scientific studies prove that electrons from the Earth also have antioxidant properties. They not only can tone down the destructive effects of free radicals, they also reduce inflammation, the culprit behind comprised health that is now linked to debilitating conditions and many chronic diseases.

WHEN INFLAMMATION GOES
ROGUE

Inflammation, by its very nature, is the body's way of beginning the healing process and affects almost every aspect of our health. But like those free radicals, when inflammation goes rogue and becomes chronic or acute, it can sabotage your health. Chronic inflammation can eventually cause several diseases and conditions, including cancers, arthritis, and more. Inflammation can and often does occur for years in the body before it is apparent or clinically significant. And it's not an older person's affliction either, as often thought. A youngster, even a toddler, can be joyfully playing and fall down, get knocked around, and allow inflammation in. Athletes, be they wannabe stars, everyday amateurs, or religious gym goers, are constantly inviting bumps and bruises. Making matters worse, much worse, inflammation begets inflammation and can have a compounding effect and long go undetected. How long it has been lurking and ravaging the body determines the degree of severity of a disease and the prognosis.

One could argue that without inflammation, most diseases would not even exist. When you realize that inflammation has been connected to just about every modern-day disease you'll better understand just how rampant it is. According to recent statistics, on average one in twelve women and one in twenty-four men have been diagnosed with inflammation-related syndromes. And these statistics don't take into account the number of undiagnosed persons suffering in silence. Diet is said to be a major cause of inflammation, but so are lifestyle factors like stress, inadequate sleep, blood sugar imbalances, depression, lack of exercise, too much exercise, and not being electron nourished—each of which can be helped by plugging back into the Earth.

CLIMB THE MOUNTAINS AND GET THEIR GOOD TIDINGS.
—*John Muir*

STAYING IN
CIRCULATION

The health benefits don't stop there though. Grounding has also been linked to the restoration of optimal circulation and the normalization of blood pressure by improving blood viscosity—the measure of the ability of blood to flow through your blood vessels. It aids in stress reduction and increases energy. It harmonizes and stabilizes our body's natural biological rhythms. It helps you sleep better. And it reduces pain. If not for all the evidence-based research that has been conducted on grounding over the past two decades, we might even call it a miracle of nature, which it clearly is. Add the fact that it's free and available everywhere you go only begins to express the far-reaching possibilities grounding has for health care today.

WHAT WE NEED IS NOT THE WILL TO BELIEVE,
BUT THE WISH TO FIND OUT.
—*William Wordsworth*

Going outside to recharge is the easiest way to clear your head, improve your memory, lift your spirits, inspire your creativity, boost your immunity, and take care of your body, without making an appointment, paying a fee, traveling far, or rearranging your how-can-I-find-the-time schedule.

You can't get much busier or experience harder workouts than star athlete, Green Bay Packers MVP Aaron Rodgers. Super Bowl champion with a line of NFL records behind him, he is a force to be reckoned with on and off the field. While there is no question that he is physically fit to meet the demands of his professional life, he amps up his health and wellness regimen with hot yoga, vitamins, diet—and sleep. A good night's sleep, in his case, one that struggled to reach the six-hour mark, was the one goal that eluded him until he found out about grounding. For a pro athlete who puts a tremendous amount of physical stress on his body, sleeping less than six hours is asking for trouble. Performance will eventually suffer, the adrenal system can take a nosedive, and immunity can be affected—making it the perfect set up for injuries too.

How did he tackle his sleep problem? You guessed it. By grounding.

"I always try to get a little grounding in," he said. His first line of defense is a grounding pad, specially made to plug into the Earth's surface while he lays on it indoors, inducing a restful, revitalizing sleep.

Grounding didn't just change his sleep habits. It changed his attitude toward the future. "Three, four years ago, I didn't think mentally that I could handle playing pro ball for much longer," he said, admitting that it is a huge drain on his body and mind. "But when you're getting more sleep and you're taking care of your body—and your body feels better—your mood is better. And this whole thing is more enjoyable, and more fun." Which is just what Mother Nature intended.

I BELIEVE THAT THERE IS A SUBTLE
MAGNETISM IN NATURE, WHICH, IF WE UNCONSCIOUSLY
YIELD TO IT, WILL DIRECT US ARIGHT.
—*Henry David Thoreau*

Our stress-filled times are wreaking havoc with every aspect of our daily lives. Isn't it time we paused to take a nostalgic look back at our youth, when we were free to play outside, often running barefoot without a care, and when we slept soundly after the day was done? We didn't know it at the time, but that feel-good feeling that resonated with every step on the ground was also the best thing we could do for our bodies and our health.

We can still easily feel that way today. We'll show you how in the following pages.

CHAPTER TWO

MAN BELONGS TO EARTH; EARTH DOES NOT
BELONG TO MAN.

—*Native American Proverb*

What the Natives
KNEW

Grounding is one of the oldest healing modalities in history. From ancient Chinese medicine to godlike Roman rulers and Native American tribes, early nature-bound inhabitants and holistic healers knew instinctively what was good for their bodies, what gifts were found in nature, and what steps to take to sustain them naturally.

Take a look at Roman and Greek history and you'll find that walking barefoot was a privilege of the ancient gods. The association between going barefoot and having a superhuman nature also influenced Renaissance and Baroque artists. Michelangelo's Sibyls and Prophets in the Sistine Chapel are all fully dressed, but barefoot, and Bernini's Santa Teresa is barefoot, too. Even the Bible makes reference to barefoot blessings, skin to soil, when Moses was asked to take off the sandals from his feet "for the place on which you are standing is holy ground" (Exodus 3:5).

Ancient references notwithstanding, Earth, all of it, is holy ground when it comes to its inherent health treasures. Consider the genesis of Chinese medicine, rooted in energy healing for thousands of years. Traditional Chinese medicine holds that human beings replicate the universe in that both are made up of the constant interaction of five main elements: metal, fire, wood, water, and Earth. These five elements are believed to constantly interact with all of the organs of the body as the five phases of universal qi, or the life force—the intrinsic energy that travels along pathways in the body called meridians. Good health is achieved when the interactions between the elements are balanced and flow smoothly.

NATURE, TIME, AND PATIENCE ARE THE
THREE GREAT PHYSICIANS.
—*Ancient Chinese proverb*

Eastern healing theory deems that disease occurs when the body is out of balance. Energy, if not flowing properly through the human body, will store negative patterns within it that can cause blockages. These blockages disrupt health, affect emotions, increase anxiety, deplete energy, invite pain, and trigger many other stressors that influence and lead to disease. Instead of treating the disease as is typical in traditional western medicine today, Chinese medical practitioners, then and now, looked at the body as a whole rather than as individual symptoms. They strived to prevent disease before it began.

They did it—and still do—through ancient practices like Qigong and Tai Chi, both of which allow the body to balance itself for optimal health. Qigong typically involves moving meditation, coordinating slow, flowing movement, deep rhythmic breathing, and a calm meditative state of mind. It has been popularly referred to as Chinese yoga. Qigong is an integral part of traditional Chinese medicine, along with acupuncture, acupressure, and herbal medicine.

Tai Chi, a meditation in motion, was originally a form of martial arts. Today it is practiced as a form of whole body movement that stimulates natural healing. By following age-old regimens like these, the body naturally rids itself of unwanted imbalances to efficiently function in harmony. Chinese medical practitioners also incorporate treatments like acupuncture to stimulate the flow of energy through the body by placing needles at specific points along pathways called meridians. By stimulating these points, the body's qi or vital energy, rebalances.

How does all this relate to grounding?

Grounding is all about connecting and interconnecting with the Earth's energy to keep one's body balanced and healthy. Chinese medicine is also all about maintaining a balanced energy flow to ensure a person's good health. A key principle in Chinese medicine states, "Cool head, Neutral heart, Warm belly." In Western cultures, people are often out of balance with a hot head, neutral heart, and a cool belly. Getting grounded immediately helps flip a person back into the cool head and warm belly balance naturally. Persons engaged in the practices of Qigong and Tai Chi commonly take their exercises outdoors and leave their shoes off. Interestingly one of the most important acupuncture points in Qigong practice, K-1, is located in the ball of the foot. K-1 is a major energy vortex that has the ability to revitalize body, mind, and spirit. It can be activated with acupuncture, acupressure, exercise, and grounding.

WALKING IS MAN'S BEST MEDICINE.
—*Hippocrates*

The Chinese weren't the only proponents of natural healing. Across the seas in another time and place similar ideas about healing were taking shape through the findings of Hippocrates in Greece around 400 BC. Today, acknowledged as the father of modern medicine, he is also known as the founder of holistic medicine. He was the first in his time to attribute illness to an imbalance within the body, not as an affliction caused by the gods.

THE PHYSICIAN TREATS, BUT NATURE HEALS.
—*Hippocrates*

This wise ancient Greek doctor contended that health was a harmonious balance of the body's natural elements. Disease, he maintained, results from their disharmony and imbalance. Hippocrates placed great emphasis on strengthening and building up the body's inherent resistance to disease. For this, he prescribed diet, exercise, massage, hydrotherapy, and sea bathing. The Hippocratic tradition emphasized environmental causes and natural treatments of diseases, the causes and therapeutic importance of psychological factors, nutrition and lifestyle, and independence of mind, body, and spirit. In addition, it underscored the need for harmony between the individual and the social and natural environment. Hippocrates himself was a stellar example of his natural health philosophy: he lived a good long life of close to ninety years, which back then was more than double the average life expectancy.

WE MUST TURN TO NATURE ITSELF, TO THE OBSERVATIONS OF
THE BODY IN HEALTH AND IN DISEASE TO LEARN THE TRUTH.
—*Hippocrates*

Medical knowledge in the Middle Ages appears to have stood still. While the ancient Romans, Greeks, and Egyptians pushed forward medical knowledge during the height of their empires, the momentum they started began to stagnate in Europe. Superstition and religious beliefs trumped the inherent holistic wisdom of their predecessors. As a result, it did not develop at the same pace until the late 1600s and 1700s. That's also the time when European explorers crossed the seas in search of new lands to conquer.

According to expedition leaders to the new world in the 1700s, the natives they encountered were "undoubtedly the finest looking, best equipped, and most beautifully costumed of any others on the continent . . . their atmosphere is pure, which produces good health and long life . . . ." That they were tremendously rugged, "going about their days often without shoes and in their stockings" gave expedition members pause, including renowned Swedish botanist Peter Kalm, who was commissioned by the Royal Swedish Academy of Sciences in 1750 to travel to the North American colonies on a scientific fact-finding mission. "It may puzzle belief to conceive how such lusty bodies should have their rise and daily supportment from so slender a fostering . . . with nature their best clothing. In them the old proverb may well be verified: *Natura paucis contenta* [translated, it means "nature is content with just a little"] for though this be their daily portion, they are still healthful . . . ."

Were they grounding back then? Wholeheartedly and unequivocally yes. The proof was in their looks and physiques reported by Kalm: "They are all very well formed with handsome bodies and good faces . . . all alike have very straight legs and no belly . . . ." That they were also "among the happiest races of Indians I have met with" speaks volumes about what it means to be truly grounded.

We asked Dr. Lewis Mehl-Madrona, MD, PhD, of Cherokee and Lakota heritage, the author of several books, including the acclaimed Coyote trilogy, Coyote Wisdom, The Power of Story in Healing; Coyote Healing, Miracles in Native Medicine; and Coyote Medicine, Lessons from Native American Healing and a practicing physician with more that twenty years experience in clinical, teaching, and research, what the Native American Indians knew about grounding.

He laughed, as did the tribal elders he posed the same question to, who according to Mehl-Madrona, "laughed hysterically" at the notion of having to coin a phrase for this natural act. "We never had a term for it. No one talked about it. It's elemental. We just did it. I think you have to be non-grounded to think about grounding."

Which is exactly the point. The Indians knew firsthand the healing benefits of sitting on the ground, touching trees, and walking everywhere they needed to go. In traditional Native American cultures they were always active. They hunted, fished, trapped, and canoed. They lived and thrived outdoors, enjoying robust health without the interference of the chronic sedentary ailments that plague many today. It wasn't until they were relegated to the reservations where they stopped actively engaging with nature did chronic diseases and inflammatory disorders begin to emerge and plague their health.

Diabetes was first diagnosed in the Indian culture in 1932. It had never been seen before. Why? Because they had never been sedentary before.

"Sedentary lifestyles and staying indoors have a profound effect on the spirit and our overall health," says Dr. Mehl-Madrona. "Walking for as little as thirty minutes can have a huge impact on health."

> TO TOUCH THE EARTH IS TO HAVE HARMONY WITH NATURE.
> —*Oglala Sioux*

He continued.

> "The modern world gives people the option of not moving. You can get away with it for a while, but eventually it will stop you in your tracks. I was treating an elderly patient on the reservation who was suffering from diabetes, hypertension, and pain in her knees. I encouraged her to begin exercising by walking, a little each day, to help improve her health. As difficult as she found this 'prescription' initially, she started walking every day. That simple act lowered her blood sugar enormously, reduced the pain in her knees, and eliminated the need for her hypertension medication. All by just walking. The studies about recoveries like these are enormous. And it's simple medicine. If you don't move, you die. And if you move with nature all around you, that's when real health takes over.
>
> "Our ancestors in all indigenous cultures knew that we belong to the Earth, as much as any rabbit or deer. Even our movements, our footsteps, honor the Earth. And the Earth honors us back. We are changed by a power that is not our own, an energy that transcends and understands us and engulfs us in its blessing. When we are in harmony with the Earth, our cells are in harmony with us. Harmony is the music of healing.
>
> "Disharmony produced cellular degeneration, viral infection, and disease—AIDS, cancer, and so on. Never have we been so removed from

the harmony of nature as today. One of our Navajo elders, a shaman and shepherd named Hosteen Begay, thought of pavement as the curse of the *bellagana* [white man] because it prevents us from touching the Earth during the day. If we have lost our connection to the Earth, then we are not grounded, and we must endure, without protection, the lightning bolts flung our way."

"We are a part of the Earth and it is part of us," affirms Dr. Mehl-Madrona.

Native Americans also naturally loved the soil. They sat or reclined on the ground with a feeling of being close to a mothering power. It was good for their skin to touch the Earth. They wore leather hides (moccasins) or walked with bare feet on the sacred Earth. They built their tepees on the Earth, and their altars were made of Earth. This is why the old Indian still sits upon the Earth instead of propping himself up and away from its life-giving forces.

> "HEALING," PAPA WOULD TELL ME, "IS NOT A SCIENCE, BUT THE
> INTUITIVE ART OF WOOING NATURE."
> —*W. H. Auden*

Something's amiss in our present-day culture. Inactivity has given rise to a host of deadly diseases at costs that are equally as staggering. But there is an obvious solution—just outside the window. For most of human history, people worked, lived, and played outside. But recently, millions of us have completely disconnected from nature. Writer Richard Louv coined a term for this in his 2005 book, *Last Child in the Woods*. He labeled it "nature-deficit disorder."

In an interview with Brian Clark Howard that was published in *National Geographic* (June 2013) Louv stated:

> If you look at a new body of research on depression, ADD, physical health, child obesity, and the epidemic of inactivity, nature is a good antidote to all of that. I didn't coin it, but I like the phrase 'sitting is the new smoking,' because new evidence shows that sitting long hours indoors every day can have serious health risks similar to those caused by smoking. Researchers at the University of Illinois are investigating whether time in the woods could be used to supplement treatment of ADD. A 2012 study at the University of Kansas found that young people who backpacked for three days showed higher creativity and cognitive abilities. People in hospitals who can see a natural landscape have been shown to get better faster. As an antidote, we need to figure out ways to increase nature time even as technology increases. It has to be a conscious decision.

The natives knew, naturally. It's time we did the same.

CHAPTER THREE

LOOK DEEP INTO NATURE AND THEN YOU
UNDERSTAND EVERYTHING BETTER.

—*Albert Einstein*

Earth Science 101 and
YOUR HEALTH

WHY THE
DISCONNECT?

If you studied Earth science in school, chances are you can recall a few basic facts about the Earth's surface that you probably haven't thought about in years, let alone applied to your own health. And you may remember that the Earth's surface is electrically charged. You may not realize that every time you touch the ground, you are coming in contact with a constant flow of electrons that your body needs to be in balance and function properly.

Stated simply, here's why: Earth, like everything on it, you included, is made up of atoms. All atoms are made of the same three basic particles—protons, neutrons, and electrons. The difference in the number of protons and neutrons in atoms account for many of the different properties of the Earth's basic elements, like oxygen, hydrogen, and the like. The number and arrangement of electrons in an atom define the chemical characteristics of elements. One way to think about electrons is that they are in the outer shell of every atom, the virtual glue that holds atoms together in chemical bonds. A normal "happy" atom is balanced and has a neutral charge with equal numbers of positive and negative particles. Ions are atoms with extra electrons or missing electrons. When you are missing an electron or two, you have a positive charge. When you have an extra electron or two, like the surface of the ground has, you have a negative charge.

The positive and negative charges continue to attract each other like magnets. The attraction of opposite charges is the way atoms form and maintain bonds. While any atoms in a bond can get or give up electrons, their optimum state is a balanced one.

These small particles, electrons, create currents of electromagnetic energy. They can easily move from negatively charged ions to positively charged ones. While negatively charged ions have extra electrons, the positively charged ones want more electrons. The electrons can jump from one to another in an effort to achieve a balanced state.

There is a constant rhythmic flow of this kind of electrical energy in and around the Earth that is being continually replenished by the sun, lightning and heat from its always-hot molten core. In fair weather conditions, the surface of the Earth is negatively charged, letting loose with a virtually limitless supply of free, unpaired electrons floating through the ground. The atmosphere around the Earth is positively charged, due to ionization by the sun's rays. In stormy weather, most lightning arises from a discharge of electrons from a thundercloud as they race back down to Earth.

These electrons that radiate from the surface of the Earth and water have access to us through the conductive surfaces of our skin. When our skin touches the Earth, it enables the transfer of electrons into our bodies, helping us to mollify our own supply of what are called free radicals.

Free radicals, as mentioned earlier, are atoms or molecules that have a single unpaired electron in their outer shells. With a single electron, free radicals are voracious scavengers, stealing or "oxidizing" electrons from healthy tissues, and thereby damaging them. Over time, oxidation sets off a chain reaction that damages a cell's structure and its ability to function. This damage is often cumulative and can contribute to aging and a variety of degenerative and chronic diseases. At low concentrations, free radicals can help the body defend against pathogens—external invaders like bacteria, viruses, or other disease-causing microorganisms. However, when free radicals multiply, they can overwhelm one's body and become wildly out of balance—they go crazy and attack the body's "good guys"—one's healthy tissue.

That's when we need antioxidants. One of the primary ways antioxidants protect against free radicals is by donating an electron to the free radical, so it no longer acts as a hungry scavenger stealing electrons from our tissues. As medical practitioners through the ages discovered, the human body performs most optimally when it is balanced. Today's healers supplement their barefoot wisdom with evidence-based studies that affirm that a body is balanced when grounded—when there is an adequate supply of electrons available to it.

A naturally potent source of antioxidants, the Earth's energy field helps create and sustain a stable internal bioelectrical "environment" in the body. While the diet of the week promises to ante up our antioxidants, the Earth's charged surface is the most commonly overlooked and most readily available option.

Okay, but what does an electric charge on Earth's surface have to do with our health?

All living things are electric beings, each capable of generating electricity. We all have electric currents inside of us that allow our nervous systems to send signals to our brains to control our heartbeats, send blood coursing through our veins, and keep us rhythmically in tune with nature's circadian cycles. Think about those tests you may have been given at the doctor's office like an electrocardiogram (EKG) or an electroencephalogram (EEG), which measure the electrical activity of your heart and head respectively. Both use external sensors on our skin to measure electrical activity occurring internally within our bodies.

Marine animals, eels, and sharks, among them, have sensory pores in their skin that enable them to detect electrical fields created by their prey as they swim in the water. This happens every time they move! Back on land, bees differentiate between vibrant and dying flowers when landing to pollinate by sensing the strength of the flowers' electromagnetic field.

We also interact with electric fields and electric currents outside of our bodies. So, if you are electron deficient, like so many of us are due to our modern-day environment and lifestyles that deter daily direct contact with the Earth, your body may have a positive electric charge. Because positive charges attract negative charges, interacting with the Earth will enable your body to absorb its abundant electrons, thereby returning your body to a more balanced, healthier state. Standing in the shower, rinsing with running water or playing in a waterfall, if you are lucky enough to be on an exotic vacation, can also replete your electron flow.

> NATURE'S PEACE WILL FLOW INTO YOU AS SUNSHINE FLOWS
> INTO TREES. THE WINDS WILL BLOW THEIR OWN FRESHNESS
> INTO YOU, AND THE STORMS THEIR ENERGY, WHILE CARES WILL
> DROP OFF LIKE AUTUMN LEAVES.
> —*John Muir*

Our ancestors naturally took advantage of this Earthly healing resource by staying in close constant contact with nature for thousands of years. That is until progress and its attendant modern-day technologies and cultural mores stepped in.

We mentioned that Native American Indians first felt the unnatural effects and resultant debilitating diseases of "progress" when they shed their outdoor lifestyles, leather-soled moccasins included, for a sedentary existence indoors. Other cultures followed suit in dress and daily life, transitioning from farms and countrified towns to man-made urban environments and cityscapes at the turn of the twentieth century.

Interestingly, the evolution of shoes played a big part of man's disconnect from nature, but it didn't happen until the mid-twentieth century when advances in rubber, plastics, synthetic cloth, and industrial adhesives allowed manufacturers to streamline the shoe-making process. When mankind first walked atop the Earth, they made "footbags" of leather that protected their feet from rocks, debris, and cold. The world's oldest shoes were laced cowhide sandals, found in an Oregon cave in 1938, that dated back sometime between 7000 BC and 8000 BC. In Scandinavia, shoes found with the frozen body of Ötzi the Iceman, who lived around 3300 BC, were made from bearskin, deerskin, and bark-string net. Ancient Egyptian sandals were fashioned from papyrus and palm leaves. The Maasai in Africa wore rawhide sandals. In Asia, rice sandals were all the rage; in South America, leaves from the sisal or Yucca plant covered their feet. Leather shoes were the material of choice for shoemakers in Europe and the Americas from the mid-eighteenth century to the mid-nineteen hundreds, ending a reign of naturally conductive footwear that enabled the wearer to benefit from connecting to the Earth's surface when walking outside. Now with most shoes made with soles of plastic, rubber, and other insulating materials, we are walking away from one of the world's best health care plans.

Urban landscapes too contributed to man's disconnect from nature. As cities paved over the dirt beneath our feet, they used materials that effectively blocked us from the Earth's subtle, always replenished healing energy. These include wood, carpet, vinyl, and asphalt, any nonporous surface material that effectively blocks us from the ground.

On the job front, high-rise offices skyrocketed the barriers between workers and their walks on terra firma. Computers, cell phones, and tablets have replaced real-life adventures with virtual worlds and now distance children and adults from natural playgrounds and much-needed exercise. As well, over exposure to electromagnetic frequencies (EMFs) can also be harmful and may increase the risk of certain cancers, sleep disorders, and more. Grounding mitigates some of the effects of our constant deluge of these electromagnetic fields.

ADOPT THE PACE OF NATURE: HER SECRET IS PATIENCE.
—Ralph Waldo Emerson

It's time to come down to Earth and get grounded again. There are ways to get back to nature and its healing resources without moving back to the woods. We'll tell you more in the following chapters, beginning with the studies that show just how effective grounding is when it comes to your health.

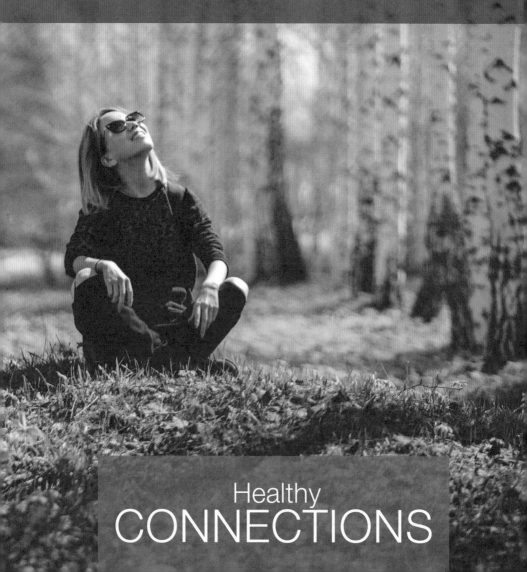

CHAPTER FOUR

IN EVERY WALK WITH NATURE ONE RECEIVES FAR
MORE THAN HE SEEKS.

—*John Muir*

Healthy
CONNECTIONS

THE PROOF, THE POSITIVES, AND
THE POSSIBILITIES

It doesn't take a scientific study to validate the feel-good effects of taking a walk outside. Spend a few minutes strolling off into the great outdoors, and you'll kick your cares to the curb. It couldn't be a more perfect exercise. It is invigorating and restorative, calming and uplifting, a mood booster and a stress buster. It has the ability to change your brain, cool tempers, soothe sadness, and make spirits soar. Effortlessly you sidestep toxic, taxing situations. Walking in nature serves as the most reliable natural prescription to mental and physical well-being.

WALK TO BE HEALTHY; WALK TO BE HAPPY.
—*Charles Dickens*

We all know the benefits of exercise are indisputable. In addition to its head-clearing endorphin fixes, you can tone your legs, trim that belly fat, and lose some of that unhealthy visceral weight that may be wrongly wrapped around your liver and kidneys. No costly gym memberships or doctor's visits here. The complementary inherent highs of walking help lower blood pressure and with a host of other good-for-your-body benefits, they can add years to your lifetime and life to your years.

The medical evidence is compelling. Akin to the proverbial apple a day for your mental health, researchers have found that walking literally changes your brain, improves short-term memory,[1] rejuvenates mental energy,[2] and enhances cognitive function.[3] It heightens levels of attention in children and in individuals who live in urban areas. Groundbreaking cognitive neuroscience studies on brain scans prove that even microbursts of time spent stepping out in nature can increase creativity and decrease the pattern of thinking that is associated with the onset of mental illnesses like depression.[4]

Apple cofounder Steve Jobs, innovative to the core, was known for his walking meetings. Facebook's Mark Zuckerberg often holds conversations on foot. So did President Harry S. Truman, the father of psychoanalysis Sigmund Freud, English author Charles Dickens, and Aristotle who famously lectured students in his Peripatetic school on walkabouts. The Greek word, *Peripatetic* means "of walking" or "given to walking about." Why would these thought leaders banish the boardroom, close the classroom, and ditch the office? They claimed to do their best thinking when walking, escalating creative inspiration with every step.

Doctoral candidates at Stanford University gave legs to this theory through a series of experiments designed to gauge creative thinking. The overwhelming majority of participants were more inspired while walking, with the creative output increasing by an average sixty percent over their sedentary cohorts.[5]

> I HAVE TWO DOCTORS, MY LEFT LEG AND MY RIGHT.
> —G. M. *Trevelyan*

Walking is not limited to just stirring creative juices alone. Studies published in the *Journal of the American Academy of Ophthalmology* have suggested that walking guards against myopia or nearsightedness in children[6] and can even stimulate the production of anti-cancer proteins.[7] Scientific findings indicate that walking in forest environments benefits the human immune function, improves mental health, and reduces the risk of early death—lowering mortality rates from cancer, lung, and kidney disease.[8]

The outdoors helps us age gracefully, too. Research published in the *Journal of Aging Research*, (Volume 2013) revealed that participants, (ages seventy to seventy-seven), who spent time outdoors every day reported fewer complaints of aching bones or sleep problems, than those that stayed indoors all day.[9]

Dr. Mehl-Madrona told us about a ninety-nine-year-old Native American woman who lived alone on an isolated Indian reservation in Arizona. She lived in an abandoned railway boxcar without plumbing or electricity, with very few of the basic amenities we all take for granted. Her days consisted of tending her sheep, walking everywhere in her old leather moccasins, and thriving on food she grew. When she visited her doctor, she was lively, good-natured, and clearheaded. She had sharp mental acuity and exuded overall well-being that belied her advanced age. How did she defy the odds and stay the picture of health despite her living conditions? "She walked in beauty," Dr. Mehl-Madrona told us, explaining that it's a long-held belief of Native American culture that when you maintain a close connection to the Earth and live in harmony with the environment, you can achieve an ideal state of well-being and health.

IF YOU TURN OUT TO WALK IN WINTER WITH COLD FEET, IN AN
HOUR'S TIME YOU WILL BE IN A GLOW ALL OVER.
—*Madame Gout to Mr. Franklin (Benjamin Franklin)*

Clint Ober, an inspiration to many, launched the modern day Earthing movement. Along with Dr. Stephen Sinatra and Martin Zucker, their book, *Earthing: The Most Important Health Discovery Ever!* brought grounding and Earthing into the public eye. Packed full of evidence-based analyses and observations, their work "rediscovered" that reconnecting with the Earth is more that a proverbial walk in the park. It is life altering.

Jim Oschman's research findings stress that the human body's connection to Earth's natural energy is essential to health. "We know that many of the most common and debilitating health disorders and diseases are partly or entirely energetic in nature. They are, therefore, difficult to prevent, treat, or even comprehend without embracing the role of energy in the person's health," he attests.

IF YOU WANT TO FIND THE SECRETS OF THE UNIVERSE, THINK IN
TERMS OF ENERGY, FREQUENCY, AND VIBRATION.
—*Nikola Tesla*

Among the most common, he notes, are arthritis, heart disease, cancer, stroke, chronic obstructive pulmonary disease, osteoporosis, and diabetes. The increasing prevalence of inflammation contributing to these and other twentieth-century ailments point to evidence of a disturbing epidemic largely caused by our urban lifestyles and "a modern disconnection with the Earth's surface," explains Oschman.

Current studies not only illustrate that grounding helps reduce inflammation and foster a more normalized state of well-being, they document what our forefathers have known since the beginning of time.

The effects of connecting directly to the Earth's surface include the following:

- Reduces inflammation
- Improves sleep
- Alleviates pain
- Accelerates healing
- Induces relaxation
- Increases heart rate variability
- Reduces blood viscosity

Where's the proof? You'll find it in a comprehensive array of multidisciplinary research and clinical studies that reveal that the electrically conductive contact of the human body with the surface of the Earth produces intriguing effects on physiology and health. Researchers like James Oschman, Stephen Sinatra, Gaétan Chevalier, Richard Brown, Karol Sokal, and Pawel Sokal, continue to experiment, study, publish, and celebrate these scientific hypotheses through meticulous research with measurable outcomes. You can find peer-reviewed studies and mainstream articles listed on Earthinginstitute.net and www.grounded.com. Additionally, accumulating real-life experiences from holistic healers, wellness practitioners, and the medical community support their findings with indisputable stories and testimonials, many of which you'll find within this book's pages.

Still skeptical? You're not alone. Even Dr. James Oschman was doubtful of the seemingly too simple concept of grounding at first. But with a scientist's curiosity and an incessant search for answers that comes with his profession, he set about to study and interpret the research that was conducted by the Earthing scientific team.

It is interesting to note that skeptics tried to discredit the researched findings of the Earthing scientists pointing out the fact that the research was sponsored by the same company that makes the grounding or indoor Earthing systems. But, as a point of fact, Karol and Pawel Sokal, physicians from Poland, discovered the same phenomena as Clint Ober did, at about the same time. Their studies were done entirely independently. They confirmed the value of Earthing.

Their research began by conducting sleep studies with people who suffered from some form of insomnia. Findings indicated that sleeping grounded improved the quality of sleep.

Many of those who experienced improved sleep by grounding also reported feeling less pain from injuries or conditions like arthritis. As more feedback was gathered, it appeared that many other uncomfortable or debilitating conditions were partly or completely mitigated by grounding the body during sleep, including a host of disorders related to exhaustion, stress, and often times, resulting anxiety. Pain reduction from sleeping grounded has been documented in a controlled study of delayed onset muscle soreness (DOMS). Sleeping grounded is the first intervention ever discovered that speeds recovery from the pain of DOMS.

There is also significant evidence that painful conditions are often the result of acute or chronic inflammation—conditions caused in part by highly reactive molecules known as free radicals. Free radicals, normally found in the body, are also generated by the immune system in response to injury or trauma. Because of its clinical significance, inflammation has become the subject of intense biomedical research, particularly in recent years. This research has documented a relationship between chronic inflammation and virtually all chronic diseases, including the diseases of aging. Inflammation produces heat that can be measured with infrared medical imaging. A study using this approach revealed rapid reductions in inflammation at the same time as pain was reduced.

How does grounding the body reduce inflammation? The logical explanation is that grounding the body allows antioxidant electrons from the Earth to enter the body and neutralize positively charged free radicals in sites of inflammation. If this is correct, one would expect changes in the blood chemistry profiles and white blood cell counts associated with inflammation. Such changes have been documented. Moreover, changes in rhythms of the stress hormone, cortisol, and in melatonin, "the hormone of darkness," have been documented. Finally, rapid stress reduction has been confirmed with various measures showing rapid shifts in the autonomic nervous system from sympathetic to parasympathetic dominance and normalization of muscle tension, completing the cascade of effects of grounding the body on inflammation, pain, sleep, and the debilitating consequences of stress and lack of proper sleep: Grounding leads to a reduction in inflammation, which reduces pain, improves sleep, reduces stress, and improves health.

Their research didn't stop there. Further studies they conducted graphically illustrate how grounding reduces inflammation by increasing zeta potential (a measure of the electrical force that exists between red blood cells) by improving blood flow and reducing blood pressure. Research of the effects of grounding continues today on sleep disorders, chronic pain, cortisol levels, and the implications of grounding in the aging process and immune response. The results can be summarized in a single statement: Connecting with the Earth is easy and can have many first aid benefits by reducing and even preventing chronic inflammation.

The good news prevails. You can experience the positive health implications and possibilities yourself by getting grounded, feeling, at the very least, a little bit better with every step.

CHAPTER FIVE

EARTH LAUGHS IN FLOWERS.

—*Ralph Waldo Emerson*

Change Your Life
NATURALLY

Grounding is all about taking little steps that can make a big difference in your life no matter where you live, work, or play. The Earth's gifts are available all around you, boosting spirits and benefiting bodies by nature's mere presence alone. In the past few decades a growing number of well-researched books by doctors and scientists have affirmed the connection between nature and human health, including the positive effects that just looking at nature can have on depression, immunity, vitality, productivity, creativity, memory, and cognitive functions. In their book, *Your Brain on Nature: The Science of Nature's Influence on Your Health, Happiness, and Vitality,* Eve Selhub, MD, and Alan Logan MD, cited that spending just twenty minutes amidst a vegetation-rich area of nature improves emotional strength, perspective, and vitality.

A study published in the *Journal of Epidemiology and Community Health* found that people who lived within a half-mile of a green space experienced less anxiety and depression than those living farther away.[1] Studies by Roger Ulrich of the University of Delaware and others stated that simply viewing nature can encourage healing and lowers the amount of the stress hormone cortisol in the blood significantly.[2] A must read is Richard Louv's book, *Last Child in the Woods: Saving Our Children from NatureDeficit Disorder.*

The healing effects of a natural view are increasingly being understood in stressful environments such as hospitals, nursing homes, and military sites as well as for people who work in windowless offices—that's lots of us. Studies also reveal that nature is an effective means of relieving stress and improving well-being. The Japanese call the grounding effect of looking at trees *shinrin-yoku*, which means "forest bathing." They actually prescribe this for patients as part of medical care. Just getting outside to take a walk encourages the body to release serotonin and natural endorphins we call happy hormones.

NATURE IS MY MEDICINE.
—*Sara Moss-Wolfe*

It goes without saying that living in suburbia, out in the country, near a forest, close to the water, or next to parkland offers endless opportunities to restore yourself. But even if you reside in a concrete jungle or can't get outdoors easily from your insulating high-rise perch in the city, there are steps you can take to get grounded. One of the best things about grounding is that it is accessible almost anywhere, at any place, and at any time.

TO BEGIN, BEGIN.
—*William Wordsworth*

While some natural settings are better than others, grounding spots are virtually everywhere in nature. "To me, if healthy grass is growing outside over a layer of soil, it's connected to the crust of the Earth, and that's all it needs to be," says physician Laura Koniver. An author and renowned expert on natural healing and grounding, Laura's research and professional experience affirm its role in bettering health. She adds that beaches are among the best places to get the most benefits because the moisture from the ground acts as a conductor. Laura is quick to add that a person can reap grounding rewards from grass, sand, rock, dirt, and even concrete. "There is literally nothing—from PMS [premenstrual syndrome] to jet lag to dementia to weight loss—that does not positively respond to time spent grounding," she adds.

"Lean against a tree, hold onto a limb and feel your circulation rev up within minutes. Holding onto a branch even if you are bundled up with the heaviest winter clothes will still ground you as effortlessly as laying in a bathing suit on the sandy beach of an ocean shore," says Koniver.

People have reported a warming sensation in their hands and some a tingling in their feet; here's one for the tree huggers! Their faces often instantly brighten with color from better blood flow. Even if you don't feel any sensation at all, rest assured your body is benefitting. The Earth's energy is a subtle one—no jolts required.

> IN THE SPRING, AT THE END OF THE DAY,
> YOU SHOULD SMELL LIKE DIRT.
> —*Margaret Atwood*

If you don't have a yard, see if you can secure a plot in a city or town garden and get your fingers dirty in the soil while you plant, weed, or pick flowers. Or sit with your back against a tree or lie down in a grassy area of a park or patch in a playground. Of course, skin to soil contact is ideal but wearing natural fiber, like cotton, linen, silk, or wool touching the ground will also allow the flow of this nourishing energy.

Schedule a nature hike, picnic in a park, or relax in a plant-filled courtyard, and get as close to the greenery as you can. Cities like Paris and New York have created tree-lined promenades and aerial greenways to give their residents and tourists alike, a place to walk with nature. Animals, as well, benefit from paw-to-Earth outings. Just watch a puppy with an injured foot make a beeline for the ground. Animals instinctively place an injured body part against the Earth.

If you can't touch nature, you can most assuredly find a cement sidewalk. As counterintuitive as it may seem—concrete being a solid, hard surface—it's conductive. Concrete is just reconstituted sand and water and it allows for the transfer of electrons, too. Don't shy away after a stroll in some drizzle or after a rainfall either—damp concrete is a good thing. Conductivity is enhanced by moisture. Sealed surfaces, such as glazed tiles or stone, along with vinyl, carpeted, and wood floors are insulators and don't allow electrons in. And because roadway asphalt is fabricated from petrochemicals, it's out, too—so no jay walking. Chances are you won't be walking barefoot on city sidewalks to get the optimum boost you need, but today you can don special grounding shoes that enable you to tap into the ground when doing so.

Footwear with electrically conductive soles provides grounding. While leather, a breathable hide, is conductive, it has become very difficult to find shoes with pure leather soles. Some that boast this oft regarded luxury, however, are glued to the insoles that touch your feet with insulating, non-conductive adhesives. Moccasins with smooth leather bottoms certainly work but can be slippery on moist surfaces and are limited style-wise, not best for the meeting in the boardroom or night on the town. Plastic and rubber can be made conductive through special formulations, but ordinarily, they are not. Because the soles of most shoes are made from synthetic materials, you won't be able to receive the health benefits of grounding while you are wearing them. Why is this important? Because your feet have the most nerve endings per square inch of skin than any other part of your body.

The Chinese identified a major energy point on our feet some 3,000 years ago. According to studies by leading acupuncturists at the Modern Institute of Reflexology, "the K-1 (kidney) Meridian point, the only meridian origin on the bottom of the feet, holds a reputation for dramatic healing response." Today you can find grounding footwear that is engineered to ground the K1 point of the foot, enabling the wearer to benefit from the most direct energy flow while wearing the shoes outside.

HOW DOES THE MEADOW FLOWER ITS BLOOM UNFOLD?
BECAUSE THE LOVELY LITTLE FLOWER IS FREE DOWN TO ITS
ROOT, AND IN THAT FREEDOM BOLD.
—*William Wordsworth*

If you practice yoga or Tai Chi, you may not be aware that these mind and body exercises have been historically and traditionally done in bare feet. The central focus involves "growing a root" that allows for the opening of a pathway between the Earth and the body by way of the feet. Certain yoga poses also employ a sense of grounding, allowing your body and mind the opportunity to release anxieties and physically join you to the Earth. With yoga as a grounding mechanism, you rely on both your mental focus and connection to the Earth in order to experience a balance of the mind and body.

There are four yoga poses that are particularly advantageous in grounding both mentally and physically. These are Mountain Pose, Tree Pose, Downward Facing Dog, and the Child's Pose. Many practitioners believe that establishing a connection through these poses and absorbing the Earth's energies keeps us nurtured, alive, and energized. As importantly, it reminds us of the value of connecting with nature.

Guided meditation can also help to align your energies with the Earth's energies so that you feel calm, refreshed, and at peace. There are many meditations that are used in grounding, some are performed inside; others are practiced outdoors, sitting on the ground or perched against a tree. Plants and trees have their own energy fields and you can absorb this energy in a positive and revitalizing way for your whole being. One of our favorite meditations is to lie on the ground, head down with one ear to the Earth and to listen softly for ten minutes. The brain settles, the body relaxes, and aches and pains can begin to diffuse.

Documentary filmmaker and wildlife preservationist, Steve Kroschel is today a die-hard supporter of grounding; in his words, "It was a life saver." He lives in Haines, Alaska, population 1,700, where his lifestyle is all about the call of the wild. As part of his normal daily routine, he walks everywhere, regularly hiking into the wilderness and into town, chops wood, and hauls buckets of water, feed, and bales of hay to the orphaned arctic wildlife he cares for at his rehabilitation center. In wintertime, he adds snow shoveling to the mix—and a lot of it. In an average year, Haines logs in more than eighty-three inches of the white stuff, but during the 2011–2012 season, it received a record-breaking 360 inches! "That's when I injured my back," said Steve.

"The number-one injury sustained after a snowstorm is lower-back strain," according to Henry Goitz, MD, an orthopedic surgeon at Henry Ford Hospital in Detroit, and a spokesman for the American Academy of Orthopaedic Surgeons (AAOS). "That's when a muscle gets over-tensioned and tightens," he explains. "If it over-tightens, it's almost like a spasm, and that gets very painful."

"The pain in my back was overwhelming," Steve remembers, wincing at the thought. "I couldn't sleep at night and was finding it difficult to move during the day. I was in agony." Forced to stay inside and rest, he found himself listening to a health and wellness program on the radio. Serendipitously, the topic that day was grounding, and Steve was all ears.

"At that point, my pain was so severe that I was game to try anything that could help. When I heard that you could alleviate aches and inflammation from lying on the ground, I decided, what's to lose, as far-fetched as it seemed." But where in the midst of an Alaskan winter, especially one that was defying all predictions with the twenty-plus-foot record-making snowfall in one storm, could you find bare ground he wondered. Then it hit him!

"In spite of the subzero temperatures, I crawled underneath the cabin buck naked. I felt tingling at first but after twenty to thirty minutes I felt oddly warm. When I went back into the house, I slept soundly for the first time in weeks." But even more surprisingly, Steve awoke pain free. "I attribute it to nothing else but grounding," he proclaimed. I shared my story with my neighbors, many suffering from a host of aches and ailments. They were skeptically enthusiastic about exploring this natural remedy. I arranged for them to get grounding products they could use indoors."

The results manifested in all manner of healing for the folks in Haines. So surprising were these results that we went to Haines to interview these new converts, hearing how grounding helped with myriad ailments, from alleviating a woman's discomfort from arthritis, to eliminating a disabled fireman's back pain so he could lift again, in addition to treating insomnia and sleep apnea for several residents. As well, many a bedfellow was happy to silence the melodic sound of snoring. Even, Karen, the orphaned moose Steve was caring for, responded, instinctively heading to the grounding mat he had hooked up for her.

The results were so astonishing Steve was compelled to make a documentary film about this phenomenon. As vividly seen in his first documentary, *GROUNDED*, he continued to experiment with plants to test the grounding theory. Plants that were wired to a grounding connection thrived while the others died almost immediately.

> HUMAN SUBTLETY WILL NEVER DEVISE AN INVENTION MORE
> BEAUTIFUL, MORE SIMPLE OR MORE DIRECT THAN DOES
> NATURE BECAUSE IN HER INVENTIONS NOTHING IS LACKING,
> AND NOTHING IS SUPERFLUOUS.
> —*Leonardo da Vinci*

Because weather and whereabouts can limit our access to nature, commercially manufactured devices that connect to the energy of the Earth, via the grounding port in electrical outlets, are becoming even more readily available. These indoor-use products are designed to promote conductivity of the natural electron flow while sleeping, engaging in exercise, or indoor activities. There are even conductive grounding pads for connecting your body to the Earth while sitting at your desk at work. Watch your furry little friends make a beeline for these mats.

> NATURE CAN DO MORE THAN PHYSICIANS.
> —*Oliver Cromwell*

Even if you're really skeptical about the health benefits, it's something that's free to try, and it sure can't hurt! Ideally, Laura Koniver recommends grounding every day for at least ten minutes, but stresses, "You can never overdo it."

CHAPTER SIX

FITTING A WALK INTO A BUSY LIFE CAN BE
CHALLENGING, SO I SUGGEST WALKING RATHER
THAN DRIVING TO WORK OR TO RUN ERRANDS
AS OFTEN AS YOU CAN—IN OTHER WORDS, THINK
OF WALKING AS ALTERNATIVE TRANSPORTATION..

—*Andrew Weil, MD*

Expert
CONNECTIONS

Everybody does it. Walking is probably the one and only exercise people have done since they were kids and, barring any severe illness or disability, still do every day, regardless of where they live or how they live, even if they don't know that they're exercising. Among its virtues: Walking is low impact, low maintenance, low risk, and high in rewards. It's not only one of the easiest and healthiest habits a person can have, it works in your best interests for a lifetime.

There's something about the rhythm of walking that puts body, mind, and soul in synch. We know that it's heart healthy and brain balancing, thanks to leading medical experts who walk the talk. Among the luminaries who have stepped into the spotlight, they include Andrew Weil, MD, and Mark Fenton, who literally wrote the manual on walking called, *Walking: The Ultimate Exercise for Optimum Health*. In addition, scientist Katy Bowman, author of *Move Your DNA: Restore Your Health Through Natural Movement,* callsd walking a "superfood." Osteopathic physician Dr. Joseph Mercola, a *New York Times* best-selling author who has been hailed a wellness game changer for his insights on effortless healing, and integrative cardiologist Dr. Stephen Sinatra, author of *Revelations from Heaven and Earth* and a dozen more noteworthy change-your-life health books, are enthusiastic proponents of the benefits of walking and grounding.

Amazing things happen if you put one foot in front of another and keep going for as little as thirty minutes, three times a week. Studies have shown that walking reduces the risk for developing hypertension, type 2 diabetes, high cholesterol, and coronary heart disease. It can lower blood pressure, weight gain, and joint pain. It improves moods, immune function, and memory. Researchers at the University of Exeter have found that it eases "chocolate lust" and sugar cravings. The American Cancer Society praises it for its ability to reduce the risk of breast cancer. Doctors applaud it for all of the above and then some, sharing stories of how their patients lived fuller lives, were sick less often, stayed more active, cleared their heads, and socialized more—all because of their prescribed daily walks.

The medical and scientific experts we talked with about walking and grounding went one step further. They stressed the value of walking in nature. They cited the medical benefits of regularly interacting with nature—touching a tree, swimming in the sea, digging in the dirt, building sandcastles on the beach, lying down on a grassy knoll, skin to soil. What they found through their research studies and real-life patient protocols points to the healing nature of the Earth as a treatment table for virtually every manner of disease and distress.

Howard Straus, grandson of alternative health pioneer Max Gerson, grew up with the notion of nature as physician, an all-knowing resource that puts the power of self-healing at everyone's hands—and feet.

"Grounding is not a matter of belief," he told us, personally attesting to nature's medicine chest. "I have blood tests to prove it."

Afflicted with a hereditary form of anemia since childhood, Howard was used to his famous family's concern and prescriptive treatments to alleviate his condition. "They supervised my eating habits and nutritional intake to correct it through diet, continually monitoring my blood work and energy level. Because I never had much stamina and lacked the energy to do what other kids my age were doing, I became a bookworm." A bookworm, we might add, who grew up to be a nuclear physicist.

Howard lived this way for years, accepting his compromised vitality and limited athleticism, until his mother, Charlotte Gerson, founder of the Gerson Institute—a San Diego-based non-profit organization dedicated to supporting her father's alternative therapies in the treatment of cancer and other chronic diseases—was contacted by Earthing pioneer Clint Ober.

> "Would she consider grounding her house?" he asked. Clint had heard about my mother's work and decided that her endorsement of the relatively new concept of "Earthing" would be worthwhile in getting the word out about this natural healing resource. Figuring she had nothing to lose, she agreed.
>
> She let him ground everything in the house, from the beds to the pads he placed near her computer. And she felt so good with all the changes, that she sent me a king-size grounding sheet for my bed. I hooked it up and slept well for the first time in years.

Howard wondered if the grounding did anything for him since he had no obvious problems other than his anemia. "After three days, it occurred to me that I had this anemia, so I decided to have a blood test (CBC) for a 'before' picture, then do it again after a month, for an 'after' picture, and compare the two. I had years of blood work, thanks to my mother's constant vigilance on my anemia. The blood test after three days of sleeping grounded was, for the first time in seventy years NOMINAL. In other words, all the parameters were right down the middle. There were no indications at all of any kind of anemia! THREE DAYS! And the parameters have remained good ever since (well over five years)."

This science person went on to research the history of connecting with the Earth through the ages, and found, like we did, that early people had no idea of this now modern-day coined concept, "that was just how they lived. They slept, stood, sat, and walked on the ground in bare feet or natural leather-soled shoes. They didn't think it was a solution. It just was."

What was also key, he pointed out, "They didn't have anything to disconnect them from the Earth.

"That all changed in the 1940s and 50s when we began to see signs of Earth Deficit Disorder."

Like his grandfather and his mother, both staunch natural health advocates, Howard champions back-to-Earth movements that have the potential to combat man-made illnesses, taking the opportunity to share his findings and experiences on the speakers' circuit, on his Voice America radio show, *The Power of Natural Healing*— and on his daily constitutional to his mailbox.

I noticed one of my neighbors, who looked to be in his late fifties, well built and tall, limping along the path like he was a cripple. I didn't know him personally, but I was concerned about his mobility issues. So I asked him why he was walking like that. He told me that he had terrible pain in his joints, and some days he couldn't even get out of bed. As we talked, he told me that he played professional football in his twenties but suffered from arthritis as the years progressed. He tried surgeries, medication, and other doctor-prescribed treatments that ultimately didn't work. He looked painfully resigned to his fate.

I told him that I had a solution that might just blow him way. "You have a backyard," I said. "And I assume you have a lawn chair. Take your shoes and socks off and spend thirty minutes there reading a book."

"Then what?" he asked. I said, "That's all. I'm going to let the results speak for themselves. Just do it."

"So you're telling me to sit in a chair with my bare feet on the ground for thirty minutes and I don't have to do anything else," he said, shaking his head.

I nodded, waved, and headed off toward home. The next time we saw each other he comes running across the parking lot, obviously not crippled anymore. He said, "Almost as soon as I put my feet on the ground, my pain was gone." True story. His name is Dennis Pearson, and he played with the Atlanta Falcons in the late 1970s and now, when he can't be barefoot like he is on his daily walks on the beach, he wears grounding shoes wherever he goes.

Howard went on to talk about his friend, Millie, who lived in Carmel, a naturally feel-good destination if there ever was one. She was in her eighties and had lost her daughter to rheumatoid arthritis. She also suffered from arthritis, debilitating at times. A big fan of barbershop quartets, she would regularly open her home to Howard and his musical mates for rehearsals.

"We would rehearse in her living room," said Howard, who recalled how happy Millie was to hear them sing and how delighted they were to be served home-baked cookies and tea at every rehearsal. But one day, after welcoming them inside, Millie told them how sorry she was that she couldn't serve them that day and to help themselves. Her arthritis was clearly challenging her every movement.

I suggested that we sing outside. I would bring a chair out for her, and would she come out and take off her shoes and enjoy the music? She looked at me like I was a little bit crazy, asking an eighty-year-old woman to sit outside in bare feet. I promised her that she would love it. We sat her in a chair on her concrete patio, a conductive surface for grounding, and we serenaded her for a couple of hours. Afterwards, Millie got up as though she didn't have a care in the world, and out came the tea and cookies. When I asked her how her arthritis was, she flexed her hands and said, surprised, "It's gone."

Always a man of science, Howard invites other scientific minds on his show to discuss a wide range of alternative healing therapies, remarking that the beauty of their findings and recommendations is that not only do they work, but they're abundantly available in nature. And in the case of grounding, it's also free.

Jim Oschman recalls how he was first introduced to grounding by chiropractic doctor Jeff Spencer. A former Olympian cyclist with advanced degrees in health and wellness, Jeff worked with athletes in nearly every professional sport, including Olympic gold medalists, drivers for Nascar, and cyclists for Le Tour de France. Jeff called upon Jim to substantiate the effectiveness of grounding with regard to its healing capabilities.

"I flew from Boston to California to meet Jeff. I looked at a study Clint Ober had commissioned on cortisol response to sleeping grounded. An anesthesiologist involved in the study had initially declared potential grounding effects impossible, saying, 'I think you're wrong, and I'll prove it.' Not only could he not disprove it, he became one of its early white paper advocates. That was enough to peak my interest as a scientist and researcher." Today Jeff regularly provides his hard-riding cyclists with grounding recovery bags to speed their muscle recovery, reduce tendonitis, and keep their spirits high.

That first study on cortisol proved to be a game changer for Jim as well. Cortisol is a naturally occurring steroid hormone that influences the release of substances in the body that cause inflammation. At night, cortisol levels should decrease, keeping time with the Earth's diurnal rhythm, to enable sleep. When someone's cortisol is out of sync with this cycle, they are often reduced to counting sheep. As well, chronic stress causes continuously elevated cortisol levels; these can impact wound healing, can reduce bone formation, (a precursor to osteoporosis,) and can weaken the immune system. The researchers found the physiological results of that early grounding study to be encouraging, noting that the subjects who slept grounded exhibited normal day-night cortisol rhythm, their sleep improved and their pain and stress levels declined.

Subsequent grounding studies proved to be extremely important on several fronts. Over the past twenty years during which he has assessed the positive effects of grounding, Jim has seen a big shift in the health care community as people are coming together to find workable solutions to the chronic disease crisis that's plaguing our lives and our economy. Currently more than $2.3 trillion or approximately seventy-five percent of our annual health care budget is spent on chronic disease and is arguably the single biggest drain on our economy.

> THINK ABOUT IT: HEART DISEASE AND DIABETES, WHICH
> ACCOUNT FOR MORE DEATHS IN THE US AND WORLDWIDE
> THAN EVERYTHING ELSE COMBINED, ARE COMPLETELY
> PREVENTABLE BY MAKING COMPREHENSIVE LIFESTYLE
> CHANGES. WITHOUT DRUGS OR SURGERY.
> —*Dean Ornish*

"Chronic disease is highly expensive to treat and debilitating on every level, and inflammation has been proven to be a precursor to chronic disease. In fact, all chronic disease begins with inflammation," says Jim. And connecting our feet to the ground to halt out-of-control inflammation is what grounding is all about.

We all agree that nobody wants to get a chronic disease, but too few of us know how to keep from getting one. In the twenty years that we have been studying the results of medical research, through blood tests, thermal imaging, visual analog scales, blood pressure cuffs, molecular electronics, and patient testimonies, we have documented the positive steps we need to take to keep inflammation in check.

The main hypothesis is that connecting the body to the Earth enables free electrons from the Earth's surface to spread over and into the body, where the electrons can have antioxidant effects. These mobile electrons build an antioxidant microenvironment around an injury site effectively walling it in preventing reactive oxygen species (ROS) delivered by white blood cells from causing "collateral damage" to healthy tissue, and preventing or reducing the formation of the so-called "inflammatory barricade." This prevents so-called "silent" or "smoldering" inflammation from forming.

Sounds simple, and it really is. Jim suggested that if ambulances had grounding pads to place on a person's injury as soon as possible after the damage occurred, they could conceivably prevent the inflammatory response and those PAC-MEN from getting out of control.

Other ways he suggested to stop the onslaught of free radicals in an injured body or in a healthy body that needs to be recharged is to take a shower. We know that showering helps us feel better, but he says the water can and does refresh your body's electron supply. Just fifteen minutes of getting grounded can charge your mitochondria and fill your electron reservoirs in case you fall down during your daily walk or run.

Studies on blood viscosity also showed that a person's blood gets thick if they're not grounded. When you're grounded, the electrons stick to the surface of your red blood cells so they don't clump. When you're grounded, your blood flow speeds up and courses through your arteries and veins unimpeded, like it is supposed to.

Concludes Jim in a 2013 white paper study he presented on blood viscosity with Gaétan Chevalier, PhD, Stephen T. Sinatra, MD, FACC, FACN, and Richard M. Delany, MD, FACC, "Increased blood viscosity in the general population may be a predictor of cardiovascular events because of its influences on hypertension, thrombogenesis, ischemia, and arthrogenesis. Unfortunately, blood viscosity has become a forgotten risk factor and is rarely measured in clinical practice. Grounding appears to be one of the simplest and yet most profound interventions for helping reduce cardiovascular risk and cardiovascular events."[1]

THOSE WHO THINK THEY HAVE NO TIME FOR EXERCISE WILL
SOONER OR LATER HAVE TO FIND TIME FOR ILLNESS.
—*Edward Stanley*

Jim cautions that grounding is not a cure for chronic diseases, but it often takes the pain away and relieves other symptoms that are a bane of these illnesses. His research will continue he promises, with the hope of seeing grounding become the norm in people's everyday lives—their homes, workplaces, and when they are outside, basically everywhere people go in their daily routines.

CHAPTER SEVEN

THERE ARE ONLY TWO WAYS TO LIVE YOUR LIFE.
ONE IS AS THOUGH NOTHING IS A MIRACLE. THE
OTHER IS AS THOUGH EVERYTHING IS A MIRACLE.

—*Albert Einstein*

The Myths, Misconceptions, and Downright SKEPTICS

Jim Oschman sums up grounding this way: "The moment your foot touches the Earth . . . your physiology changes."

Your blood flow improves. Your heart beats easier as it more naturally responds to the environment. Feelings of anxiety and stress melt away. The less stressed you are, the more relaxed you feel, the fewer headaches you have, the better you'll sleep, and the more energized you'll be. Higher energy levels mean more motivation, less inactivity, and more interest in taking the steps that lead to better health, inside and out. Those daily walks in the park we've been advocating also help strengthen your bones, initiate weight loss, help you heal, improve bad moods, and rejuvenate your brain as they inspire healthy lifestyles, all while fighting the underlying inflammation that can ultimately stop you in your tracks. That one simple act of grounding leads to a welcomed domino effect that benefits body, mind, and soul.

People who integrate grounding into their everyday lives are more centered, more balanced, and on track for optimum health. They have traded in their glass of wine or piece of chocolate to blunt the end of the proverbial bad day for the zero-calorie option of grounding. In addition to its inherent physiological health benefits, incorporating a walk in nature actually modifies your nervous system so much that you may even experience a decrease in anxiety or hostility. Bring a friend along on your grounding walk and you will boost your mood even more. Happy feet are harbingers of whole body health.

BLESSED ARE THE FLEXIBLE,
FOR THEY SHALL NOT BE BENT OUT OF SHAPE.
—Unknown

In spite of all the good news grounding brings, misinformation and misconceptions still exist. You may be wondering why a proven, feel good, refreshingly free healing modality that's been a part of mankind's daily regimen since the beginning of time is just now gaining ground with the public.

Explaining that people were naturally more grounded before the advent of synthetic lifestyle solutions, Howard Straus reminded us that grounding "wasn't something anyone needed to think about doing; it was something they did without thinking." There wasn't even a term for it until recently. Add the fact that as society disconnected from Mother Nature and her bounty as urbanization advanced, the concept of natural healing itself became questionable. Ironically, this was foreshadowed by the one word career advice given to Dustin Hoffman in his 1960s breakout film *The Graduate*—"Plastics."

"Traditional healing that was rooted in thousands of years of ancient practices that found cures in nature became labeled and derided as 'alternative,'" he said. "But after decades of living with the detrimental effects of what is now recognized as

'Nature-Deficit Disorder,' the pendulum has shifted back." Grounding, while never needing to be singled out as a mindful health protocol, is now coming back into the fold as an essential part of a person's overall wellness plan.

THE MOMENT ONE GIVES CLOSE ATTENTION TO ANYTHING,
EVEN A BLADE OF GRASS, IT BECOMES A MYSTERIOUS, AWESOME,
INDESCRIBABLY MAGNIFICENT WORLD IN ITSELF.
—Henry Miller

Many doctors today are turning to age-old treatments like acupuncture and meditation as part of a larger integrative approach to health. With the rise in chronic disease and the associated pain syndromes that often go along with it, the medical community has taken note of how ancient Chinese practitioners saw the mind and body as connected and inseparable. Traditional medicine practices are built around the intangible ideas of wellness, vitality, and healing. Their prescription for treating illness incorporated ways to balance the body and unblock energy flow so the whole body could return to its natural state of equilibrium. Modern medicine, on the other hand, has typically placed more emphasis on acute illnesses and not on the idea of preventing the disease from taking hold in the first place.

"The goal should be to enhance and optimize the body's natural function," says Mark Hyman, MD, a best-selling author and the director of the Center for Functional Medicine at the Cleveland Clinic, in an interview with Jennie Rothenberg Gritz and published by *The Atlantic* in a June 2015 footnote.[1] If a patient comes to see him with a combination of health issues, like high blood pressure, eczema, and gastrointestinal problems, he tries to figure out how they are all connected and then identify the causes. As we know, these all happen to be inflammatory disorders. In such a case, he says, "Once we realize this, all the medical boundaries start to break down, and we're able to focus on restoring balance."

We talked to Judy Brooks, Public Broadcasting System radio show host and cocreator of *Healing Quest*, a program based on the booming interest in integrative health and natural approaches to well-being. Her show, now in its thirteenth season, subscribes to the philosophy that healing is a lifelong journey toward wholeness. To validate and underscore its importance, she interviews guest speakers well versed in the subject, along with the show's regular guests, including Dr. Mehmet Oz, Deepak Chopra, Judith Orloff, and other leading experts, who share their insights on natural ways to stay healthy. They touch on alternative medicine, spiritual relaxation, nutrition and diet, physical and mental exercise, and socialization, as they explain the studies, the symptoms, and the successes of natural healing.

WHEN YOU REALIZE NOTHING IS LACKING,
THE WHOLE WORLD BELONGS TO YOU.
—Lao Tzu

"Anything that brings nature back into your life is a good thing," says Judy Brooks, adding somewhat incredulously that it took her a long time to get the media to pay attention to nature's healing possibilities. "Alternative medicine was not a popular topic twenty years ago," she said, "but in the last ten years, it has seen a surge in popularity as stories about energy medicine and its success in treating illnesses have become newsworthy.

"Keeping your body balanced as nature intended is key to maintaining your health," she shared, "and grounding is a dirt cheap and effective way to do that."

World-renowned body-mind medicine expert Deepak Chopra has written more than eighty books on alternative medicine, including the recent *Radical Beauty* with nutritionist Kimberly Snyder, where grounding is one of the six pillars. A grounding advocate, Deepak agrees that it can reduce levels of chronic pain and lower levels of the stress hormone, cortisol.

Kimberly looks at grounding from a beauty perspective, and recommends it for its anti-aging properties as well. The fact that grounding reduces stress, lowers blood pressure, and aids in the circulation of nutrients and oxygen through improved circulation ensures "beautiful, healthy skin and hair." It also helps mitigate the effects of osteoporosis, which "could do wonders for bone health and help us maintain an upright graceful structure." And don't overlook wrinkles. Better circulation can help keep them at bay, too.

Take a page out of their book and you'll find them recommending naps in the grass so that you wake up feeling "radically recharged," and inviting friends for walks in the park so grounding becomes a part of your daily routine."

"It seems so simple," write the authors, "but remember that some of the most beautiful things in life are truly simple. Nature is so healing to us; all we have to do is reach out to her and she will help us heal from the inside out, while your beauty benefits as well."

KEEP KNOCKING AND THE JOY INSIDE WILL EVENTUALLY OPEN
A WINDOW AND LOOK OUT TO SEE WHO'S THERE.
—*Rumi*

Too good to be true? No such thing as a "free lunch?" The skeptics aren't convinced.

What do skeptics say about grounding? While they are more prone to dismiss the overall concept of alternative medicine as a whole, they find it difficult to believe that the simple act of grounding is beneficial to one's health.

Many question both the studies and the stories, equating them with wishful thinking or woo-woo science and doubting the effectiveness of grounding as a healing source.

They maintain "the research has no merit because it has not been published in peer-reviewed journals," and the "research is worthless because it has been funded by an organization that also sells grounding projects." We are not sure we understand why critics would make such statements without checking the facts, so we'd like to set them straight here. Of the twenty-one studies posted online by the Earthing Institute (www.Earthinginstitute.net/research), eighteen have been published in peer-reviewed journals including the ones most read by scientists worldwide. Many of the studies were placebo-controlled, double-blind, which means that the results cannot be construed as "fake news."

What's more, they suggest that grounding is a moneymaking ploy, rooted in a manipulative move to sell the public on a baseless idea and gimmicky products. Grounding products were developed in response to the studies' findings that connecting to the Earth provides significant health benefits. The products enable the housebound to access the Earth's healing energy. Gimmicky? Hardly. They have been tested by researchers and scientists who found them to be safe and effective and beneficial to the user, not to mention the countless unsolicited testimonials from satisfied consumers.

Some skeptics claim that grounding is harmful, particularly indoors, and that it can turn the body into an antenna that attracts EMFs. Not only is there no evidence to support their claims, grounding offers some level of protection against EMFs. Part Chicken Little thinkers, part doubting Thomases, many people are prone to suspect anything that sounds too good to be true. We get it.

But as the skeptics challenge the documented findings of health experts and people helped by grounding, we would ask them to step back a moment and consider how they feel when they take a walk outside, sleep restfully all night long, wake up refreshed, and have more energy to get through the day. We ask them to imagine walking away from their aches and pains, taking a breather from stress and anxiety, and enjoying time away from technology and tension. While they reject the premise that nature can heal, we suggest that they spend a day at the beach, feel the sand in between their toes; go for a swim in the ocean or a freshwater lake; stroll, shoes off, on dew-dropped grass on an early morn; or kick off their shoes and lay down in a wildflower meadow on a warm summer day. We invite them to dig in the garden, gloves off, planting seeds in soil, nutrient rich and naturally nourishing. If they don't yet embrace the premise of reconnecting with nature or think it foolish to hug a tree, perhaps they would have a seat in a park, book in hand, leaning against a tree, and feel their worries wither away.

Natural health care is not about concocting magic potions. It's based on the premise and the promise that actual healing is really possible. From hundreds of medicinal plants, herbs, and trees to life-giving landscapes and settings that have the power to soothe, restore, and revive, there is wisdom in nature that goes deep and has stayed powerful and true since the beginning of time. Grounding, safe, evidence based and chemical free, enables you to tap into that wisdom, whenever and wherever you are.

CHAPTER EIGHT

What Grounding
MEANS

TO ATHLETES,
TREE HUGGERS, AND
NATURE LOVERS

Grounding, by any other name, is still grounding. Whether advocates call it Earthing, tree hugging, daily constitutionals, barefoot bliss, mindfulness, or more, grounding offers a wealth of healthful advantages.

Grounding helps football legend Aaron Rogers sleep soundly and retired NFL pro Dennis Pearson quell his arthritic aches and pains. Elite cyclists, Tour de France contenders, turn to grounding for race recovery and healing advantages. Grounding-aware fitness enthusiasts walk, hike, and head outside to allow Earth's energy to do the healing work while they work out.

Athletes especially need to maintain that extra boost of energy that grounding supplies for optimum performance. The cells responsible for turbo-charging their bodies are called "mitochondria," regarded as the "powerhouses" of cells. The mitochondria in cells throughout our bodies are responsible for creating ninety percent of the energy needed to sustain life and support organ function. When mitochondria malfunction, organs start to fail—people get sick.

Mitochondria are responsible for producing ATP or adenosine triphosphate. This is the designated driver molecule that runs all processes in the body that use energy, including muscle contraction, secretion, nerve transmission, etc. When the body is electron deficient, there are not enough electrons to operate the electron-transport chain in mitochondria and you don't have much energy. This is why experts like Jim Oschman tell athletes to spend fifteen minutes barefoot before an event. It's a great way to make sure there are plenty of electrons for ATP production and for control of inflammation should they fall down or have some other injury.

SPORT IS A PRESERVER OF HEALTH.
—Hippocrates

Olympic gold medalist rower Adam Kreek first learned about grounding from performance trainer and TV producer Bob Babinski who was helping Adam prepare for his role as a special analyst to cover the Olympic games in Brazil for Canada in the summer of 2016. Bob was demonstrating his airport trick, a test of will, power, and magnetic attraction exhibited by someone who is truly grounded. Lest you think we are going off course here, let's go back to the dictionary definition of "grounded," which explains it two ways: One, it is defined is as being well balanced and sensible, a phrase used to used to describe a person who has a good understanding of what is really important in life. Two, it's presented as an electrical circuit that is connected to the Earth. And perhaps a third colloquial meaning that most of us know very well, grounded can mean a time-out or loss of privileges that teenagers experience (*eek!*—even radio silence from texting friends).

Bob's definition of grounding is not too dissimilar to the dictionary definitions. "Grounding is all about focus, awareness, and self-confidence, feet planted firmly on the ground to enable an unobstructed energy flow," he explained. "People who are truly grounded are relaxed and comfortable with who they are and exude an air of calm and confidence that draws others to them. They embody a naturally balanced body/mind connection that is purposeful and strong, easily absorbing any arrows of doubt that may get them off course." His take on grounding has evolved into a practiced technique that helps professional athletes, journalists, reporters, and others who perform their jobs in the public eye to stay calm and composed in the face of fire.

Imagine if you were asked to address an audience of thousands, their attention glued to your every word—and your body language, clothes, hair, looks, expressions, fidgets, and everything else that is on display as you stand bravely before them. You've never done this before, but you are determined to act cool and collected as if you were intimately chatting with an old friend in your living room. You never let on that the don't-blow-it look on your host's face is enough to send you running, or that you are worried about a personal matter, or any of the untimely distractions you must ignore because the world is watching and counting on you to deliver.

"When you're grounded, you can not only handle any situation like a pro, but you can perform your personal best as if it's the easiest thing in the world," said Bob, explaining that in a grounded state people are fully relaxed and not tensed up. When he is teaching his grounding technique to his clients, he has them stand with their feet firmly planted on the ground. Then he asks them to focus on the connection between the ball of their feet—where that energy-opening K-1 meridian point is— and the ground, finding perfect balance, and becoming body-aware and focused. He asks them to visualize something that induces an emotion they would like to feel when they reach their goal, shutting out any negative thoughts or doubts that could otherwise impact their performance. And he asks them to think about what is happening to their abdominal areas as they begin to breathe fully and naturally, without constriction. "Being grounded is the best place you can be," he stresses.

He advises his clients, most of them with driven, Type-A personalities, to devote ten minutes a day on themselves, often suggesting that they spend time outdoors in nature, taking a walk, going for a swim, or doing something they enjoy doing. All of it is part of his goal to affect the mind-body awareness that is key to success—and grounding. He says the terminology doesn't matter. Whether you are outside connecting to the Earth or inside visualizing something that makes you feel good and takes the stress away, the concept of grounding is effective, healing, and attractive.

Does he practice what he teaches? You can count on it. "I am a runner. I meditate and I practice my form of visualization," Bob conveyed, "often doing two of them at once." Meditation puts the mind and body in its most relaxed state. Visualization is very popular with the Olympic athletes he works with. They use it to rehearse their performances, and it helps with goal setting and winning. It puts them in an optimal state of mind. Bob reinforced that this is also what grounding does. Bob visualizes a cherished family memory, a moment captured in time when he and his family were swimming in a little cove on a secluded Greek Island. He experiences bliss every time he thinks about it. The perfect picture of grounding if there ever was one.

Adam Kreek grew up in the great outdoors, a fan of grounding way before anyone told him it was healthy for him. He recalls that going barefoot always just felt good. As an adult, he feels the same way, adding that it now takes on an almost spiritual significance as well. Whether he's practicing a sport, working in his shared office or just enjoying time off, bare feet is his footwear of choice, giving him energy that's almost palpable.

"You can't really measure it, but in blind placebo studies, walking barefoot definitely has an impact on your mood and energy," he said.

While training for his second Olympic games, Adam remembers rowing alone in a single boat near the mud flats of San Francisco Bay. "I pulled my boat off to the side, got off the boat, and began running barefoot through the mud flats. The ground was smushy clay, and I felt like I could run forever. As I look back at it now, I was absorbing the power of the Earth and it was awesome."

Adam recalls another memorable grounding moment that he experienced on his honeymoon in Labrador when he and his wife were exploring the wilderness near Churchill Falls. "We stood on bedrock that was over a million years old, and I vividly remember feeling more balanced and more connected than ever before." It was a moment of "remarkable pleasure, a truly magical experience" that he attributes to the grounding.

"It's not surprising that moments like these have almost a spiritual connotation," said Adam as he spoke of the ancient warrior traditions of Haka dancers of New Zealand and Kung Fu martial artists. "Contact with the Earth is integral to the practice of these time-honored warrior arts. The athletes stand with bare feet firmly planted on the ground and hold their space. They wave their arms at their opponents to try to disrupt their energy and break their power. Once you make that connection, Earth to energy, it's not easy to let it go."

LET'S TAKE OUR HEARTS FOR A WALK IN THE WOODS AND
LISTEN TO THE MAGIC WHISPERS OF OLD TREES.
—*Author Unknown*

Dr. Lewis Mehl-Madrona hugs trees not because he thinks they need TLC, but because it's beneficial to his health. Long touted as hippy dippy, tree huggers, or forest bathers, Mehl-Madrona believes trees offer an abundance of healthful benefits as they sustain Earth on every level. Before you presume that forest bathing requires practitioners to strip down and wash themselves *au naturel* in a wooded stream, this practice is more like a mobile grounding meditation that as you walk, allows you to take in the forest atmosphere, combat stress, and find peace.

A swim in the sea can also improve your mood and health, leaving you refreshed, restored, and grounded. Hippocrates first used the word "thalassotherapy" to describe the healing effects of seawater. Among several benefits, swimming in the ocean is purported to improve circulation, promote overall well-being, and hydrate your skin, not to mention the inflammation-fighting connections enhanced by the water's conductivity of Earth-bound energy into your body.

SLEEP IS THE BEST MEDITATION.
—*Dalai Lama*

GROUNDED filmmaker Steve Kroschel, as shared earlier, found relief from his debilitating back pain by sleeping outside in winter, under his cabin in Alaska no less, not something many of us are willing to do no matter how much our body aches. But we did take notice of another study that involved a group of winter campers who also willingly made their beds on the frozen Earth for a sleep study conducted by Kenneth Wright, a professor of integrative physiology at the University of Colorado, Boulder, and senior author on a study on resetting sleep cycles. While these hardy souls were not in pain, they agreed to spend a February weekend camping in a Colorado park away from artificial light to see if their bodies' biological clocks would naturally reset in tune with Earth's circadian rhythms. You may remember a similar study in which the research team explained how cortisol levels normalized when people slept grounded; the results of this study, conducted for a different purpose, underscored their findings. Along with documenting how much they slept, Wright kept track of people's circadian rhythms by measuring their levels of the hormone melatonin, which regulates wakefulness and sleep. He found that his campers, each sleep deprived to some extent before their weekend under the stars, exhibited no signs of jet lag after sleeping as nature intended. [1]

TO KEEP THE BODY IN GOOD HEALTH IS A DUTY . . . OTHERWISE
WE SHALL NOT BE ABLE TO KEEP OUR MIND STRONG AND CLEAR.
—*Buddha*

Many traditions honor the Earth for her power of nurturing. In Buddhist traditions the Earth is used as an example of equanimity and great patience. No matter the refuse that's dumped on the Earth, Mother Nature takes it in and recycles it—well, almost all of it. The Earth is a model of how anything that occurs can be transformed through patience and equanimity. And just as it can be transformed at the level of Earth, so also can it be at the level of energy and mind.

Shamanism stems from nature itself and its practices advocate tapping into the power Mother Earth has to offer, not just for the health of the individual but the health of the entire community as a whole. Rhode Island shamanic healer and teacher Linda Hogan, author of *Walk Gently Upon the Earth*, has practiced grounding with her clients for decades. She embraces the bounty that's found in nature and unquestionably credits the Earth for its endless healing energy.

"We were once wild and one with the Earth. Some of us were fortunate to start off our lives running wild through woods and meadows. Others spent our childhood in the city and may not feel the same connection. It is never too late to make this connection to the Earth. It is what sustains and energizes us, but most of us no longer remember this. We are moving so quickly in today's world that our experiences are blurred. We need to slow down so that our senses will awaken and our hearts will open. When we learn this and reconnect to nature, we are able to receive her energy and the many gifts she has for us," says Linda.

THERE IS A WAY THAT NATURE SPEAKS, THAT LAND SPEAKS.
MOST OF THE TIME WE ARE SIMPLY NOT PATIENT ENOUGH,
QUIET ENOUGH, TO PAY ATTENTION TO THE STORY.
—*Linda Hogan*

Nature physician Dr. Laura Koniver believes there are few ailments that can't be helped by grounding. She emphasizes that you can list conditions from A to Z and find that grounding will help mollify each of them in some beneficial way.

CHAPTER NINE

83
P2-4AC

15.0 cm MI 0.9
Gen Tis 1.1
[2d] G78/71 d

FA4/P90
HAR/FSI0
[C] G50/0.80 kHz
FA5/F1/8
TDI

Amplitude (V)

S-T→
ment

T

U

S-T-
interval

2.5

Time (s)

BAREFOOT WISDOM
From A to Z

You may remember hearing the saying, "Mother knows best." You may have even heard it from your own mother as she was dispensing her pearls of wisdom and you half-listened as you rolled your eyes. But you might want to pay attention now. When it comes to the range of ailments Mother Nature can help, it seems that long-standing adage still holds true. We're not surprised, given the ills that await when we disconnect from her healing presence. And as varied as the conditions are, as mentioned before, at the very heart of them is chronic inflammation.

Different from acute inflammation—the body's proactive healing response to infections, wounds, and tissue damage—chronic inflammation means long-term micro-inflammation at the level of the cells, an unnatural unfocused assault on your healthy cells and tissues that can last for several months and even years. This type of inflammation does not look like that swollen knee you got after a hard run or that egg-sized bump on your head after a bad fall. You can't feel it or be tested for it. It is a silent enemy that lurks unseen inside your body. Left to run amok, it can eventually cause diseases and conditions, including some cancers, rheumatoid arthritis, atherosclerosis, periodontitis, allergies, and mood swings.

There are literally hundreds of illnesses caused by inflammation and numerous more autoimmune diseases that trigger bad-for-your-body chronic inflammatory responses. We've included a guide here to some of the most common conditions associated with inflammation. Grounding is one of the best natural inflammation fighters there is, so it just might be the right therapeutic step for people dealing with any of the following diseases.

What follows below are the benefits of grounding for many different medical issues that are common in our lives today. Read on to see that you can add grounding to any treatment strategies or medical therapies that have been prescribed to you.

ALLERGIES: According to the Centers for Disease Control and Prevention, allergies are the sixth leading cause of chronic illness in the US. It is estimated that more than 50 million Americans suffer from allergies each year, with associated medical expenses exceeding $18 billion each year. And the numbers keep growing.

All allergies involve inflammation. Simply stated, an allergy is an overreaction of the body's immune system to relatively harmless substances like pollen, dust, chemicals, certain foods, pet dander, and the like called allergens. When the body comes into contact with them, it responds as though it's under attack, releasing antibodies and triggering inflammation. Reactions include sneezing, itching, coughing, and swelling and can range from mild to life threatening.

Everything on Earth that can be eaten, inhaled, or touched is a potential allergen. Whether or not it negatively affects you depends on your individual genetic profile and how your immune system is responding. While genetic factors play a big role in allergies, lifestyle, diet, and physical environment are important as well because they define what the body's immune system must detoxify and process on a daily basis.

Why are allergies on the rise?

The AAAAI (American Academy of Allergy Asthma & Immunology) suggests that ". . . living conditions in much of the world might be too clean and that kids aren't being exposed to germs that train their immune systems to tell the difference between harmless and harmful irritants."[1] Think of all those kids staying inside with their high-tech toys instead of playing outside as generations of children did when getting dirty was just a normal part of childhood.

"Let your kids play in the dirt," advises Stuart Levy, microbiologist at Tufts University School of Medicine, explaining that an overly hygienic childhood can raise a child's risk of asthma, type 2 diabetes, dermatitis, and Crohn's disease. The promising news is that prevention is also possible—but only if you start young. "Get your kids dirty early," suggests Eric Macy, MD, an allergist-immunologist affiliated with Kaiser Permanente San Diego Medical Center. "Once you're sensitized, there's no way to undo that. But if you grow up somewhere like on a farm, the probability that you will be allergic to anything is basically zero. Being too clean is not good."

The National Wildlife Federation says that due to climate change, environmental allergies will worsen for approximately 25 million Americans.[2] This is due to allergen triggers such as ragweed that grows faster and produces more pollen under increased carbon dioxide levels. Other effects of climate change include the increase of allergic asthma attacks due to an increase in air pollution and pollen production in cities. As a result of these environmental changes, the American College of Allergy, Asthma, and Immunology says, ". . . hay fever or seasonal allergic rhinitis lasts up to three weeks longer than it used to, and the further north you live, the longer you have to wait for relief."[3] It is crucial to note and remember that climate change is not just about environmental sustainability; it is also human sustainability.

Researchers also concur that more people are seeing stronger reactions to substances that normally should not cause problems. Changes in the global diet and gut bacteria are considered to be the strongest influencing factors.

The outdated solution to try to avoid allergens is increasingly difficult. Lifestyle and dietary modifications are now thought to be great first steps in treating allergies. The easiest step to take to keep allergies in check? Dr. Laura Koniver says, "Go outdoors and get grounded. The overall reduction of inflammation in your body after just ten to twenty minutes of direct contact with the ground will reduce or completely eliminate your nasal congestion and inflammation, and is an important way to combat your seasonal allergies."

ARTHRITIS: Part swelling, part pain, part stiffness, arthritis is all about inflammation. The term arthritis refers to more than one hundred diseases and conditions affecting the joints. It comes in various guises as it does its destructive work, deteriorating bone cartilage and derailing joint mobility as it does in osteoarthritis, or insinuating itself into your every waking hour with joint stiffness and swelling in your fingers, wrist, hips, and knees, along with many more related degenerative disorders that involve inflammation as a direct cause or by-product. The most common type is osteoarthritis, along with gout, lupus, and rheumatoid arthritis, which can affect multiple organs and cause widespread symptoms. Arthritis often occurs with other chronic diseases as well. Statistics reveal that close to fifty percent of adults with heart disease or diabetes and one-third of people who are obese also have arthritis.

At last count, in a study conducted by the Centers for Disease Control and Prevention in 2015, more than 54 million adults had some form of arthritis. The numbers vary by state with the barefoot beachfront paradise that is Hawaii coming in the lowest. In a little more than twenty years, that number is expected to soar past 78 million. Close to half of them will experience limitations in their usual activities due to the pain and swelling in their joints, increasing the ranks of a growing sedentary population. Those are worrisome numbers especially when you consider that arthritis can impede physical activity—and inactivity is associated with conditions like cardiovascular disease, diabetes, and obesity.

The good news is that people with arthritis can alleviate their symptoms by grounding. Scientific studies have shown that physical activity, like walking and swimming, decreases the pain of arthritis and improves function, mood, and quality of life for its sufferers. Regular exercise can help with weight loss too, not only lessening the strain placed on inflamed joints, but actually decreasing the progression of the disease. To keep arthritis symptoms in check, many doctors suggest walking or moderate exercise for at least 150 minutes per week most easily, or swimming in equal measures, both of which are key grounding activities.

BACK PAIN: It can start with heavy lifting, a fender bender, an accidental fall, an age-related condition, or any number of other everyday causes—and eighty percent of us will experience some form of back pain at least once in our lives. Currently, back pain is one of the most common reasons for medical attention in the United States, with problems often found in the muscles, tendons, bones, ligaments, discs, or an underlying organ like the kidneys. Aches and pains in the lower back can be chronic and are often caused by inflammatory arthritis, rheumatism, bone disease, or curvature of the spine. No matter where, when, or how it starts, it is painful and affects sleep, mobility, and mood. It may seem counterintuitive to consider taking a walk outside when even the slightest movement can manifest in breathtaking pain. If exercise is too much to fathom when you are in pain, simply lie down grounded to the earth, or sleep grounded.

CROHN'S DISEASE: One of many gastrointestinal diseases caused by inflammation, Crohn's disease can affect the lining of the entire digestive tract. This inflammatory bowel disease is characterized by abdominal pain, severe diarrhea, fatigue, weight loss, and malnutrition. The exact cause of Crohn's disease is unknown. However, like so many chronic diseases, it is thought to be due to an abnormal response from the immune system. In this case, food or bacteria remaining in the intestines or lining of the bowel may cause the uncontrolled inflammation that is associated with Crohn's disease. What does Greg Williams, a natural health specialist in the UK, recommend to clients suffering from Crohn's and ulcerative colitis? "I advise them to go outside and take a walk, because grounding helps to improve their health, reduce their pain, and increase their energy naturally."

DIABETES: Diabetes is the seventh leading cause of death in the United States. More than 29 million people in America have diabetes—that's about one out of every eleven people—with 86 million more considered prediabetic. Worldwide, it afflicts more than 380 million people, and the World Health Organization estimates that by 2030, the number of people living with diabetes will more than double—that's close to a billion. Those numbers are staggering, especially because this life-altering disease affects the whole body and can have serious complications. Currently, the number of worldwide deaths from diabetes is 1.5 million, and this skyrockets to over 3.7 million per year if you include the other diseases that are caused or exacerbated by diabetes.

Managing diabetes is a challenge every day, and keeping blood sugar levels in the desired range is a constant balancing act. The good news is that it can be prevented and controlled by lifestyle choices that include diet, exercise, and stress management practices like yoga, meditation, guided imagery—and grounding. Dr. Stephen Sinatra, a board-certified cardiologist specializing in integrative medicine is a pioneer in holistic treatment methods that focus on reducing inflammation and maximizing the heart's ability to produce and use energy. In his article *New Hopes for Diabetes*, Sinatra writes, "Our experience and observations over a fifteen-year period clearly indicate that grounding indeed holds great promise as a preventative and therapeutic strategy."[4]

ECZEMA: An inflammation of the skin, eczema is a common condition that affects people of all ages and races. It typically causes itchiness, discomfort, and a dry, scaly rash that can improve over time or remain chronic throughout a person's life. Treatment traditionally focuses on healing the damaged skin and alleviating the symptoms with moisturizers, topical creams, and antibiotics.

Kimberly Snyder, CN, a nutritionist and multi-time *New York Times* best-selling author says, "Stress breaks down the skin's protective barrier, which means we don't heal as well. It also compromises immunity, making you less able to defend against allergens." A grounding advocate, she recommends "getting plenty of sleep, drinking lots of water, hydrating the skin from the inside out, and employing stress-relieving techniques like yoga, meditation, and swimming," which happen to be great ways to get grounded.

FATIGUE: Being tired, short tempered, and unfocused from a lack of sleep is one thing, but fatigue is a different animal altogether. Fatigue is usually a more chronic, long-term condition than sleepiness and is usually linked to a more serious medical problem. If you feel a lack of motivation and energy and constantly look forward to crawling back in bed with the covers pulled over your head, then you might be experiencing true fatigue.

A constant lack of sleep can affect your overall health and make you prone to serious medical conditions, including obesity, heart disease, high blood pressure, and diabetes. But chronic fatigue is what scientists call "a sickness behavior," one of many caused by an inflammatory disease like arthritis or autoimmune disease. Unlike simply being tired from a poor night's sleep, chronic fatigue does not improve with rest. If you are wondering why you are tired all the time, you may have a problem with inflammation that you are not aware of. Medical researchers agree that fatigue remedies that address inflammation are key to getting your energy back. These include natural and lifestyle therapies involving nutrition, stress reduction techniques, exercise, lifestyle changes, and grounding.

Author and nutrition expert Kristen Michaelis, admittedly one uber-busy natural health advocate, suffered from extreme adrenal fatigue. She had a great diet and was taking the best supplements she explains, but her energy level was shot.

"I was instructed between the one week visits with my naturopath to walk barefoot on the Earth, swim in wild water, snuggle with my kids or pets, lean against a tree, place my feet against the Earth while I sat in a chair outside, anything for twenty to thirty minutes a day, to get me connected to the energy of something living," she said. What has happened to her since then? Her energy levels increased, and she experienced dramatic improvements in her sleep levels. Today, she has incorporated grounding into her life every day.

Our advice for fatigue: Don't get caught up in the too tired to exercise cycle. Just a simple walk in the park, barefoot or with grounding shoes, will do for starters, giving you a leg up on the fatigue that's been bringing you down.

HEART DISEASE: Heart disease is hands down the leading cause of death in the United States. The diagnosis of heart disease refers to several types of heart diseases, the most common of which is coronary artery disease or atherosclerosis. Atherosclerosis is a disease in which plaque builds up inside your arteries causing them to become narrow or blocked and ultimately impeding blood flow. If you go back to that high school science class again, you'll remember that arteries are blood vessels that carry oxygen-rich blood to your heart and other parts of your body. When they're compromised so too is your heart. You can live for years with plaque build-up but it progresses as you age and can become dangerous by the time you are in your fifties and sixties putting you at risk for a heart attack. The coronary disease associated with heart attacks is caused from the damage to the lining of those arteries.

Notes Rob Rosedale, MD, an internationally known expert in nutritional and metabolic medicine in his article, *Cholesterol Is Not the Cause of Heart Disease*, "When damage occurs to the lining of our arteries (or even elsewhere) chemicals are released to initiate the process of inflammation. Arteries constrict, blood becomes more prone to clot, white blood cells are called to the area to gobble up damaged debris, and cells adjacent to those damaged are told to multiply. Ultimately, scars, referred to as plaque, form inside our arteries. The constriction of our arteries and the 'thickening' of our blood further predisposes us to high blood pressure and heart attacks."[5]

Deepak Bhatt, MD, chief of cardiology for the VA Boston Healthcare System, director of the Integrated Interventional Cardiovascular Program at Brigham and Women's Hospital and the VA Boston Healthcare System, and associate professor of medicine at Harvard Medical School, adds, "Exactly how inflammation plays a role in heart attack and stroke remains a topic of ongoing research. It appears that the inciting event in many heart attacks and some forms of stroke is buildup of fatty, cholesterol-rich plaque in blood vessels. This combination of plaque and blood clots causes the majority of heart attacks and certain types of stroke, if the blood clot obstructs blood flow to the heart or brain."

Enter a grounding study on blood thickening, or viscosity, published in *The Journal of Alternative and Complementary Medicine*,[6] and conducted by Gaétan Chevalier, PhD, Stephen T. Sinatra, MD, FACC, FACN, James L. Oschman, PhD, and Richard M. Delany, MD, FACC. The title says it all. *Earthing (Grounding) the Human Body Reduces Blood Viscosity—A Major Factor in Cardiovascular Disease.*[7] The conclusions offer validating proof. "Grounding increases the surface charge on red blood cells and thereby reduces blood viscosity and clumping. Grounding appears to be one of the simplest and yet most profound interventions for helping reduce cardiovascular risk and cardiovascular events."

INSOMNIA: In her new book, *The Sleep Revolution*, Arianna Huffington cites the consequences of sleep deprivation—weight gain, diabetes, heart disease, cancer, and Alzheimer's among them—referring to it as "the new smoking." She writes, "All the science now shows that sleep is a huge performance enhancer. When we wake up fully recharged, our health is better, our productivity and creativity are better, and we're happier." She challenges us "to glamorize people who are fully recharged and ready to face the world."

Being unable to sleep is a relatively common issue in America. The Centers for Disease Control and Prevention consider insufficient sleep a public health concern,

estimating that upwards of 70 million American adults suffer from some form of sleep disorder. The fact that insomnia is fast becoming a public health epidemic is enough to keep us all up at night.

Writes Dr. Andrew Weil in an article published in *Self Healing*[8] magazine about sleep deprivation, "Insufficient sleep has been linked to a higher risk of Alzheimer's disease, cardiovascular disease, cancer, obesity, and lowered immunity." Not to mention the multitude of daytime distracted work-related and traffic, airline, and machinery accidents promulgated by persons operating on little or no sleep that make headlining news virtually every day. There are many known causes for those sleepless nights, with anxiety, stress, medication, illnesses, allergies, noise, poor diet, and caffeine, among them. But inflammation, the ceaseless opportunist that thrives because of our disconnected lifestyles, makes a poor bedfellow as well and is increasingly thought to be behind our debilitative wakeful nights.

A recent study in the journal *Biological Psychiatry*[9] reports that inflammatory markers were found in people who have sleep disturbance issues. Researchers found that sleep disturbance (not sleeping well or suffering from insomnia) as well as too much sleep (exceeding eight hours) were associated with increased levels of C-reactive protein (CRP) and interleukin-6 (IL-6), inflammation markers that circulate in the blood stream and are predictors of health issues such as hypertension, cardiovascular issues, and type 2 diabetes.

Michael Irwin, one of the researchers involved in this study, stated, "Insomnia and sleep disturbances should be viewed as risk factors for inflammation, along the same lines as sedentary behavior or an unhealthy diet are. Sleep behavior treatments could be a way to resolve the inflammation and to reduce the risk of subsequent diseases."

Rubin Naiman, sleep specialist and clinical assistant professor of medicine at the University of Arizona's Center for Integrative Medicine, points to research that links a lack of sleep to a rise in cortisol levels and inflammation biomarkers. And it goes both ways. "Sleeplessness increases chronic inflammation," Naiman says, "but chronic inflammation also increases sleeplessness." Our bodies should do exactly what the planet does when the sun goes down, says Naiman. "All of the heat absorbed during the day should dissipate and steadily decrease throughout the night before reaching its lowest point just before the dawn and coming back up," he says. "Sleep is a release of energy." Scientists have found that people suffering from sleep disorders don't get cool enough at night because they're inflamed. In some cases, their body temperature literally qualifies as a fever state, says Naiman.

"Go outside during the day, disconnect from your daily routine, and connect to nature," he advises, explaining that one of the main reasons for insomnia is hyperarousal. "We live in an age of velocity, speeding through our days, speaking faster than ever, and even watching TV programs paced to race. The antidote is humility."

Humility? Interestingly, as many linguists know, humility comes from the word "hummus" which means soil. So taken literally, humility means coming down to the ground, and reconnecting with the pace of nature, which goes and slows, enjoying a built-in respite from the rhythm of the day. People who are hyper-aroused don't have time for sleep and must consciously choose to slow down and start to feel life again.

Loss of sleep, even for a few short hours during the night, can trigger tissue-damaging inflammation according to new research. But before you lose any more sleep over all those painful thoughts or actual pains that hijack precious shuteye, consider what recent research has found out about insomnia and grounding.

Studies show that grounding during sleep has the ability to reduce a person's nighttime cortisol levels, resynching them with the Earth's natural twenty-four-hour circadian cycle and restoring natural sleep patterns. Not only can you sleep better and wake refreshed, you can keep fatigue, pain, and emotional stress at bay. People who sleep grounded say that their daytime energy levels increase as their nighttime pain levels decrease. How can you ensure a restorative night's sleep?

Keeping in mind that the original definition of the word "bed" refers to "a garden bed," you can always sleep where Mary Oliver did in her poem *Sleeping in the Forest*:

I thought the Earth remembered me,
She took me back so tenderly
Arranging her skirts
Her pockets full of lichens and seeds.
I slept as never before
A stone on the riverbed . . .

But you won't have to make a bed outside in the grass as Mother Nature puts you to sleep. You can choose to plug into the Earth with grounding pads and sheets specifically designed to ensure a good night's sleep.

JOINT PAIN: Long associated with aging, joint pain is a common complaint of people of all ages, whether it is related to a chronic medical condition or strains, sprains, and other injuries. Mildly irritating or increasingly debilitating, it can affect any part of your body that's connected by bones, from your ankles and feet to your shoulders and hands. It may last for just a few weeks or endlessly ache for months, making everyday movements painfully difficult. While you may manage it with medication and physical therapy, grounding is another, and drug-free, alternative that has proved its efficacy in a number of published studies and in personal stories.

Dr. John Briffa, MD, author and international speaker and a prize-winning graduate of University College London School of Medicine, is a leading authority on the impact of nutrition and other lifestyle factors on health and illness. When he first heard about grounding, like many of us, he read all the research and decided to test it out for himself. The perfect opportunity presented itself after he vaulted over a gate and twisted his right ankle when he landed on the other side. He recalled having pain in his ankle for some time after that, "Not enough to stop me walking, but running was out of the question. "

His grounding experiment started with him sitting with his bare feet on wet grass for twenty minutes. "Later in the day I noticed that the pain in my left foot and ankle had disappeared completely and has not returned since."

If you knew you could reduce joint pain simply by walking on the grass, wouldn't you take your shoes off right now? While grounding might not stop all your symptoms, it can definitely reduce the pain and stiffness that you feel every day.

KIDNEY: When inflammation turns on your body and affects your kidneys, like it does with chronic kidney disease, the effects range from the onset of cardiovascular diseases to anemia, malnutrition, weight loss, and muscle weakness. Chronic kidney disease may be caused by diabetes, high blood pressure, and other disorders we've listed here. You might feel tired and have less energy. You might lose your focus and have trouble concentrating. Sleeplessness, muscle cramping, and frequent trips to the bathroom might make nighttime a nightmare. Swollen feet and ankles, dry, itchy skin, and puffy morning eyes might keep you from venturing outside as often as you'd like, but early detection and treatment—think grounding again—can often help keep chronic kidney problems from getting worse.

A CAVEAT ABOUT LYME DISEASE

If Lyme disease is prevalent in your area and deer ticks lurk in that luscious grass, going barefoot outside to get grounded raises a red flag. To think that the bite of a tiny tick the size of a pin head can set in motion a litany of chronic inflammatory symptoms that can plague you for life is mind-blowing, especially since taking a walk outside in the tall grass can be one way to get bitten. Lyme disease is insidious and a large percentage of all the symptoms a person experiences—brain fog, muscle and joint pain, high blood pressure, headaches, and more—is due to inflammation. Over time it can damage the nervous system with a persistent presence. About fifteen percent of patients with Lyme disease develop peripheral and central nervous system involvement, often accompanied by debilitating and painful symptoms. New research indicates that inflammation plays a causal role in the array of neurologic changes associated with Lyme, according to a study published in The American Journal of Pathology.[10]

Bottom line, if you are bitten by a deer tick in an area with Lyme's disease—immediately seek medical attention. And remember, where Lyme is common—going barefoot outside is not a recommended solution! Use other ways to get grounded that we have shared throughout this book.

OSTEOPOROSIS: Osteoporosis, translated means "a condition of porous bones." Although some bone loss is a natural result of aging, accelerated bone density loss, rapid depletion of mineral content, and brittleness are not. Thankfully, doctors agree that there are steps you can take to prevent this disease. Among them, exercise, increasing calcium intake, and grounding! The *Journal of Environmental and Public Health*[11] discussed a possible reduction in the likelihood of developing osteoporosis when subjects spent time grounding. According to their studies, one night of grounding resulted in less calcium and phosphorous released through the subject's urine. The loss of these minerals over time is associated with the development of osteoporosis, so finding out that grounding is able to slow it down can mean wonders for bone health as we age.

STRESS: Stress is loosely defined as any reaction to a physical, mental, or emotional stimulus that upsets the body's natural balance. We are born hardwired to handle some stress say researchers, pointing out that it is critical for the survival of living beings. But in today's high-tech world, where time is money and there is hardly a nanosecond to stop, stress has not only become endemic, it has become an epidemic. With the constant surge of biochemicals that are naturally released during stress, "the body is slowly killing itself," says Jean King, PhD, of the University of Massachusetts Medical School. "This onslaught chips away at the immune system, opening the way to cancer, infection, and disease. Hormones unleashed by stress eat at the digestive tract and lungs, promoting ulcers and asthma. Or they may weaken the heart, leading to strokes and heart disease.

"Chronic stress is like slow poison," King observes. "It is a fact of modern life that even people who are not sensitized to stress are adversely affected by everything that can go wrong in the day." While we can't avoid stress, we can manage it. Dr. King advocates "listening to music, going for a walk, or exercising, which always puts my mind at ease. I love the water, so if I'm having a rough day I just go and look at it. I don't even have to go in; all I have to do is be near it."

Her colleagues "meditate regularly, practice yoga, go exercise, tend to the garden, hang out with family, or even just read and write. "You have to become aware of what calms you best," they agree, if you want to leave your stress behind.

THYROID DISEASE: In autoimmune thyroid disorders like Grave's Disease, the immune system mistakenly produces abnormal organ-specific antibodies that target your own healthy thyroid cells. Your thyroid is in charge of regulating your metabolism and is considered one of the most important endocrine glands in the body. It produces hormones that affect nearly aspect of life: hunger, sleep, reproduction, energy levels, metabolism, body weight, and more. In fact, every cell and organ in the body requires thyroid hormones to work normally.

The immune system malfunction behind Grave's disease causes your metabolism to go into overdrive, giving you that heart pounding, body trembling feeling that is characteristic of a panic or anxiety attack. In people diagnosed with Grave's Disease, the thyroid gland exhibits marked inflammation. One of the key components in achieving remission in Graves' disease is reducing thyroid antibodies by halting the inflammatory process.

One particular sufferer we came across during our research publicly blogged about her regimen for treating Graves' and not surprisingly, in addition to medication, it included her hands-and-knees-on-the-Earth grounding exercises. She also reports another rather simple remedy, "Hug a tree. If you are lucky enough to have a backyard, or a park nearby, you can do a similar exercise. Imagine the tree taking the excess energy for its own healing, grounding it through the roots."

VISCOSITY: Viscosity is a measure of a fluid's resistance to flow. When we talk about the blood's viscosity, we are referring to its thickness or stickiness and its ability to flow through the body. Blood with a high viscosity is called hypercoagulable; it is thick and slow moving, which increases your risk of having a blood clot or stroke. Hypercoagulable blood is the essence of inflammation; its slow blood flow impacts its ability to bring oxygen to your tissues, thereby paving the way for chronic diseases to take hold.

Research has found that grounding helps thin your blood by improving its zeta potential, which means it improves the energy between your red blood cells.

As Dr. Stephen Sinatra explains it in a published interview he did with Dr. Mercola in August of 2013, "Grounding Helps Thin Dangerously Thick Blood and Fights Inflammation and Disease,"[12] "Zeta potential is the electrical potential of solids and liquids, also referred to as electrokinetic potential. Grounding actually increases zeta potential by an average of 280 percent." Dr. Sinatra continued, "This is the most incredible discovery, because if you can increase the thinning of your blood naturally by grounding, you can fight off disease. Not only heart disease and stroke, but I'm thinking cancer, Alzheimer's, multiple sclerosis, or any illness that requires good oxygenation to the tissues."

WHETHER YOU TAKE ANTIOXIDANTS OR WHETHER YOU GET
ELECTRON DONORS THROUGH THE SKIN, WHAT YOU'RE TAKING
IN—INTO YOUR SKIN, AND TAKING IN ORALLY—IS GOING TO BE
SYNERGISTIC. IT'S GOING TO HELP YOUR BODY. . . .
GROUNDING IS ANOTHER NATURAL ENERGY THAT EVERYBODY
SHOULD DO IN HIS OR HER LIVES, BECAUSE IT JUST MAKES
SENSE. IT INCORPORATES A HEALTHIER LIFESTYLE.
—*Dr. Stephen Sinatra*

While we have covered some common conditions and diseases here, grounding can be beneficial for other aspects of health as well as disease prevention and treatment. As well, we have spoken with the experts throughout this book to get their take on their grounding practices so you can take your pick of the method that suits you and your life best.

CHAPTER TEN

ONE STEP AT A TIME IS GOOD WALKING.

—*Chinese proverb*

How To Get and Stay
GROUNDED
Wherever You Are

You've read about the history and health of our forefathers, the whys and wherefores of grounding, the studies and stories of people on the road to healing, and now you're game to get grounded.

SPLENDOR IN THE GRASS

Depending upon where you live, you'll find ample places to take a walk or plant your feet, from concrete sidewalks and wooded trails to a nearby beach, park, or your own backyard. If you're a city dweller, you may be wondering where you're going to find a sweet spot of grass that hasn't been fenced in or fancied by one too many dogs. Going barefoot on a country club lawn is one thing, but indulging in nature's bounty in an elusive patch of green in a concrete jungle besieged by grime and grit is a whole other matter. We hear you. But before you think grounding is out of the picture for you, picture this.

WAKE UP AND WALK

Imagine setting your alarm clock an hour before you normally wake up so you can take a walk outside in the morning air before the city rises. The sidewalks are virtually empty, the horns silent, the crowds not there. Put on your grounding shoes and enjoy the concrete. Remember synthetic soled shoes won't let the grounding in, but they can get you where you're going, which in this case, would be your nearest green. Bring your dog, if you have one, or a neighbor's pooch if you like, and take a walk on those concrete sidewalks around your dwelling. Unlike the asphalt used on streets, concrete is a conductive surface that enables the energy to flow between you and the Earth. The dog will heal while he heels, so that is a good thing for him, too.

Make tracks for the nearest plot of land; anywhere trees, plants and grass grow is ultimately where you want to go. Season permitting, kick off your shoes, and plant your feet on the ground—even a mere ten minutes will do. Or, touch that tree or plant, grasping a limb or a leaf and hold it for a few minutes. That simple connection, nature to you, is what grounding is all about.

MORNING SHOWERS
BRING HEALING POWERS

Perhaps you're not a morning person, and waking up is hard to do. Taking a shower helps give you that get up and go, but we recommend that you slow down and linger in the shower a bit longer. Water passing from the ground through the metal pipes is grounding too, transferring electrons with every drop. Keep the inside of your body hydrated as well. Over sixty percent of our bodies are made up of water and almost all of our body's systems rely on it. Tap into the restorative benefits of grounding, literally, anywhere there is a sink with a metal faucet (and metal pipes to the ground) just by holding on to it for a minute or two. Turning on the water, even a trickle will do, is best for a quick grounding anytime hit.

PICNICS ARE
PERFECT

There's something about eating al fresco that transports you to another time and space. Most cities and towns have parks that are reserved for simple pleasures like this, so if the sun is out and the day is warm, a park is the perfect spot for lunch or for a stop on the way home from work. Sitting on the Earth, or on a cloth or blanket made of natural loosely woven fibers so you connect with the ground, does wonders for what ails you. If you have an arthritic hip or sore knee, try to position that painful spot so that it's touching the ground. Even better, lay down for a spell, letting your entire body stay in close contact with the Earth and feel your stress melt away. Like the bottoms of your feet, your skin absorbs electrons, helping reduce chronic inflammation and the ailments it causes, including tension headaches, backaches, and more.

DISCONNECT

Even the smallest neighborhoods can be a hot bed of technology, emitting a constant flood of radiation from electromagnetic fields, cell phones, computers, and Wi-Fi—all of which assault your body and contribute to free radical stress. Grounding helps ameliorate your exposure to the harmful effects of modern-day communications, not to mention the onslaught of harmful pollution from car exhaust, cigarette smoke, fertilizers, insecticides, and more, and is critical to buffering the effects from by-products of modern life.

Disconnect from your cell phone, your iPad, and any other wireless device that relies on man-made electromagnetic fields to get powered up when you're out for a walk, in bed for the night or, optimally, as often as you can. According to Emil DeToffol, a former dentist who has spent more than twenty years researching the effects of what some call "dirty electricity," EMFs come from a wide range of sources including your TV, microwave ovens, appliances, both big and small, and even the electric meter on your house. Long-term exposure to EMFs is reported to have serious adverse effects on your health, including brain tumors, cancers, heart disease, Parkinson's, and more, so any measures you can take to protect yourself and your children will be a step in the right direction.

"In dentistry, we always took necessary precautions to keep our patients safe from radiation from Xrays by shielding their bodies with lead aprons and leaving the room ourselves when we turned the Xray machine on. We need to apply the same kind of thinking in our homes and our daily lives," he said.

Make your home your sanctuary. Turn off your Wi-Fi whenever you are not using it and don't sleep with your cell phone next to your bed. Keep that laptop out of the bedroom, too.

PLANT A GARDEN

Gardening, by its very nature, is healing. A growing body of research shows that people who spend time outside in sunny, green, and natural spaces are happier and healthier than those who don't. But the sensory experience of gardening, literally putting your hands in the dirt, digging, and helping something grow, actively fosters a sense of calm satisfaction, eases stress, and improves your mood and focus. A study conducted in Norway with people who were suffering from depression and who spent six hours a week for three months growing flowers and vegetables experienced a measurable improvement in their depression symptoms.

Other research suggests that the combination of physical and mental activity involved in gardening is not only therapeutic, it lowers the risk of developing dementia. You've heard of memory gardens? Residential facilities have found that Alzheimer's patients can walk through them without getting lost. The sights and smells of the gardens alone promote relaxation.

Many urban areas have introduced community gardens for those with a wistful green thumb. They are not only good for the growth of the plants and vegetables; they are great for nurturing your own well-being. And while you are losing yourself in the garden, studies show you can lose weight too, another health boon, Earth to you.

STOP AND SMELL THE ROSES

Do you live near a botanical garden? If so, stop in and smell the roses. We can't imagine a better place for grounding. The first true botanical garden took root at the University of Pisa in Italy in 1543, leaning then towards the study of medicinal herbs and plants, a wellness movement that soon spread throughout Central Europe. They morphed into tropical gardens during the seventeenth century, reflecting the age of international voyages to ports unknown and attempts to grow new species back home. It wasn't until the nineteenth and twentieth centuries that they became primarily pleasure gardens, losing their academic focus in favor of their cultural popularity.

Today, the 1,500+ gardens across the globe are a bouquet of science and delight, making folks aware of both the beauty and the bounty of nature. Some gardens hold classes in Tai Chi, Qigong, meditation, yoga, Pilates, even swing dancing, along their garden paths, perfect pairings for life-altering grounding opportunities.

SPEND TIME
NEAR THE WATER

*Since salt water is a great energy conductor a*nd sand is a close second, the benefits of spending time at the beach are indisputable. Whether you spend a week at the beach for your long-awaited summer vacation or you are one of the privileged who live near it year-round, it is a wellspring of healing properties. Ocean aside, mountain streams, river bends, ponds, and lakefronts also offer up nourishing strolls or a dip.

"Grounding through water is exponentially powerful, whether it's on wet grass, or on the seashore," says Laura Koniver, who continues that it can help with so many issues that derail your day.

The moment you step on the beach and take in the salty sea air, you breathe easier. For centuries people looked at the sand and surf as a fully stocked pharmacy. We bask in its ability to heal cuts and skin ailments, reduce inflammation, soothe the soul, and restore energy.

HARVEST
YOUR HEALTH

Spend a day in the country doing what the locals do. Pick berries and wildflowers in summer, apples and pumpkins in the fall, whatever is in season. Outdoor pursuits that involve interacting with nature's table is a feast for all your senses. Not only is it rewarding to choose your own ready-to-eat healthy treats fresh from the source, it's inherently healing, keeping you engaged and giving you more enjoyable opportunities to get grounded.

GET IN THE
GAME

Olympic gold medalist Adam Kreek grew up in Canada's great outdoors, spending days, then and now, going barefoot whenever he could. Not only does going barefoot feel great, he admits, "it also nourishes, strengthens, and promotes agility in our feet, ankles, legs, knees, and hips—benefits that many people are going without in today's over-shod society."

He told us a story about Barefoot Ted McDonald of *Born to Run* fame, describing Ted's feet as muscular and well-defined, unlike the long, skinny feet most of us have today. Ted is an independent athlete who has made a career out of following his own path, sans shoes. It took Ted about ten years to master the barefoot technique, and in that process he regained connectedness, mindfulness, and presence in running and body. He was inspired by the Tarahumara people who live in Mexico's Copper Canyon region. The entire tribe, men and women, old and young, run to live, and each is capable of running at least 250+ miles in a single run, without shoes. As if their running prowess wasn't impressive enough, they are not competitive and run for the joy of it in groups.

If you recall playing tag, badminton, pitching horseshoes, or catching fireflies, shoes off, on the summer lawns and sand beaches of your childhood, you might recognize that same joyful feeling from your memories. You can still find it today—growing up does not mean you can't partake in these nourishing activities.

HOBBIES
THAT HEAL

It goes without saying that integrative health pioneer Dr. Andrew Weil, director of the Arizona Center for Integrative Medicine at the University of Arizona, among many other roles, leads a very full life. The best-selling author of fifteen books on integrative health and hundreds of articles, teacher, sought-after global speaker, and mentor to more practitioners than we could count, he not only finds time for himself—a key to staying grounded—he makes the time. Dr. Weil rises with the sun, takes a morning and a sunset walk, often with dogs in tow, swims, gardens—one of his favorite pastimes and one that brings him great joy—and sticks to a diet of healthy, simple food.

Make time for your passion, whether it's dancing, painting, hiking, gardening, making music, knitting, and so many other activities that you can do just for you, and take it outside whenever you can.

GET YOUR
BEAUTY SLEEP

"We are in the midst of a sleep deprivation crisis," writes Arianna Huffington, the cofounder and former editor in chief of *The Huffington Post* and now at the helm of Thrive Global, on her website. "And this has profound consequences—on our health, our job performance, our relationships, and our happiness." What is needed, she boldly asserts, is nothing short of a sleep revolution. Only by renewing our relationship with sleep can we take back control of our lives.

"The impact on our health is dramatic," she says, adding that it includes everything from a suppressed immune system, hypertension, and obesity to haggard looks, dark circles and bags under our tired eyes, and all the unwelcome, wrinkled signs of premature aging. It is indisputable that getting grounded daily aids in sleep.

With our nonstop, over-scheduled, technologically tiring lifestyles, turning in while tuning out from all incessant chatter that runs through our minds might be just a dream. As if worrying about what we need to do or did during the day wasn't enough to ruin our night's sleep, many of us have a hard time staying away from our addicting cell phone or computer checking habit no matter the wee hour.

While camping out under the nighttime stars may be out of the question, you can still sleep grounded no matter where you lay your head.

Take the time to breathe before bed. Turn off your technology for at least thirty minutes before tuning in. Let your devices recharge in another room and make sure your bedroom is dark.

CHAPTER ELEVEN

Energy
MEDICINE
The Earth as Treatment Table

ANN MARIE'S
STORY

I was nine years old the first time I practiced energy healing. I was trying to make my shingles-afflicted grandmother feel better, so I instinctively did a laying on of hands over her body as energy practitioners do with their patients. This inspired me to continue working with energy. When I was in medical school, I would use my knowledge in energy healing to scan my patients to gain a better understanding of their energy fields, and find out what was going on and where the problems were before we actually ran traditional tests. My energy-based diagnoses picked up the location of the abnormality at times even before we had a proper western diagnosis.

Although I have since spent a lifetime practicing energy medicine and studying with internationally renowned practitioners, the concept of energy healing was naturally intuitive with me. It is, after all, rooted in indigenous beliefs thousands of years old that there is a vital force, an underlying flow of energy, both within the physical body and extending from it. Our bodies, healers, and scientists agree that we are actually part of the vast living energy field of the Earth. How we are connected to that energy field profoundly affects our vitality and our health.

I was born with a congenital defect in one of my kidneys. After years of pain and infections, I had surgery to correct the defect in the body. Despite being "cured," I still had intermittent bouts of pain, although there was absolutely no medical reason for it.

I started understanding that I was not "grounded" from so many years of blocked energy and pain. I began to work with grounding practices and began to go out and to lie on the Earth when I was in pain. The more grounded I became, the more my pain resolved. This experience allowed me to acknowledge the powerful connection between grounding and energy healing. I experimented with nature—I routinely went outside and lay on the ground and my pain would dissolve. It became a reliable way to stop or lessen the pain that I had.

Working with the Earth's energy is key to the energy healing practices I work with today. Simply stated, energy-based therapy is used to shift, clear, and balance a person's energy field and energy flow within the body. Once imbalances and disturbances are cleared and restored, a person's natural energy channels can continue their role in integrating the body, mind, and soul to promote healing. It is today considered by the integrative medical community an important paradigm in triggering a person's own healing system.

Once you work with the energy of the Earth, a symptom, illness, or pain often changes. Total healing does not happen overnight, yet symptoms change, illnesses retreat, and pain decreases.

Shamans work with the energy fields of the human body, nature, and the Earth. They read, respond to, and act in accordance with the Earth's energy, as well as with the energies of the weather, animals, the human body, and all other creatures. They see the energy of all these things as one fluent flow.

These healers connect with this energy, in essence connecting to the Earth and its energy field, the natural world, all things physical. I have learned that if we connect to the Earth's energy, we become more aware, vital, and attuned to our health and our own energy.

In traditional Chinese medicine, we are taught that a balanced healthy body should have a cool head, neutral heart, and warm hips and legs. In our society, cold feet are more the norm, as are hot heads, indicating that we Westerners are flipped. Experiences, thoughts, and emotions speed to our heads first, bypassing a pathway that is supposed to literally move through the body. When the energy doesn't circulate through our whole body, especially the vital energy that naturally flows from the Earth, we feel depleted and exhausted. We can also experience an imbalance of the nervous system, producing anxiety, depression, and an over-reactive nervous system and causing us to feel off balance, ungrounded with a low level of energy.

When my patients exhibit these symptoms, I suggest they begin a regimen of grounding exercises like toe tapping (an exercise from Qi Gong that stimulates the energy flow in the legs and is very effective for insomnia, anxiety and restless leg syndrome) to balance the energy between the body and the head and to restore their vitality. I also suggest breathing exercises while sitting on the earth and meditation outside while laying on the ground.

When chronic illness or pain is an issue, a flare up can cause a feeling of despair. We live in a "just take a pill culture"—we think that if we take a pill, we will get better. Yet this is not accurate for healing. I advise my patients to use energy techniques and grounding techniques over a specified time period, usually nine months. The difference, when we look back through the lens of time, is usually dramatic.

Grounding the body, energetically and physically, means strengthening our connection between our feet, legs, and the Earth's energy field. Doing so balances the energy flow between the body and the head, ensuring that the bulk of the energy is centered in the body. Grounding entails connecting to the Earth's field—the flow of electrons that are present and coming into the body naturally.

When we practice grounding and tap into the Earth's energy, we feel invigorated. When we are disconnected or blocked from it, we feel tired. To remain vital, we need to seek out ways to keep the energy exchange flowing. We need to make grounding a habit and incorporate practices that promote health and balanced lifestyles, like the ancient indigenous populations of Asia and the Americas did before us.

CHAPTER TWELVE

Getting Your **Hands** ... and **Feet** ...
AROUND YOUR HEALTH

SHARON'S
STORY

Have you ever heard of Raynaud's syndrome? Fortunately, not many people have. But for those of us who are plagued with this white-knuckle circulation disorder, it is something we wish we had never heard of either. A cold temperature culprit, Raynaud's causes some areas of your body—fingers or toes—to go numb in response to cold temperatures or stress. If you have Raynaud's, there is vasospasm in the smaller arteries that supply blood to your skin; this constricts circulation of the blood to your extremities. In the most severe cases, luckily not mine, this can lead to deformities, ulcers, or even gangrene.

Raynaud's isn't life-threatening, but it can impact your life. I know of women—we are more susceptible to it—who wear mittens in the refrigerated grocery store aisles, and who are chilled standing under a hot shower.

Here's what happens when Raynaud's kicks in. The affected areas of your extremities usually turn white when you first brave the cold and they start to tingle and go numb. As you warm up, your circulation improves and the affected areas turn back to red, sometimes itching.

My fingers and toes turn white when I am out and about in the cold and I quickly lose any semblance of feeling or warmth. It's uncomfortable at the very least and annoying all the time. When I finally went to the doctor to inquire about my technicolor tips, I learned that my poor circulation was a result of other health matters. I was a youthful smoker, a bad habit that continued for years until I came to my senses. You don't need me to tell you that smoking causes general adverse effects on the body, including inflammation, decreased immune function, and diseases that affect the heart and blood vessels, i.e., our body's circulation. Raynaud's was my ironic lifelong reward for trying to be cool as a teen!

While the cure lay right at my feet, literally, growing up in New England—colder than you'd like winter weather and command central in summer for Lyme-carrying deer ticks—there was no walking barefoot in the grass. Going outside for a morning walk guaranteed white fingertips and a numbing chill in my toes. Once I learned about grounding, my daily ritual changed, as did my susceptibility to the cold.

Here's how I handle my Raynaud's now. I either sit barefoot on the ground, keeping a wary eye out for an approaching critter, or more often, put on my grounding shoes and sit with my feet in direct contact with the Earth. After a short period of time, my white fingers tips come to back to life with color and the numbness subsides. More often than not, when I come back inside, it looks like I just brushed my cheeks with blush, a benefit from the increased circulation of simply going outside and getting grounded. Raynaud's, like so many chronic conditions, is no match for Mother Nature.

The more I tried grounding for my own well-being, the more determined I became to share this natural healing resource with others. In 2011, as I became immersed in the concept of grounding, the more I learned about it, the more I wanted to know, and the more I thought everyone could benefit. That was the impetus behind this book—and as funny as it sounds, it was inspired by my cold feet.

Thrilled personally to have learned how to kick Raynaud's to the curb whenever I felt a damp chill on my fingers and toes, I was inspired to make grounding attainable and accessible to everyone no matter where they live or work. As an entrepreneur, with decades of experience as a builder of life-enhancing businesses the world may or may not know it needs, creating a line of grounding shoes called *pluggz* primarily for women became a passion.

The idea behind crafting specialized grounding shoes was directly inspired by the remarkable discoveries—or better said, re-discoveries, by many of the highly regarded scientists, pioneers, and researchers included in this book. *Pluggz* were created to enable everyone to have the same grounding benefits the experts documented through their numerous evidence-based studies and research.

Pluggz grounding shoes are conductive, due to a custom formulated carbon and rubber plug embedded in the soles. These plugs enable wearers to connect to the Earth's beneficial energy—the electrons—when they walk on the ground. This includes grass, sand, soil, unsealed tile, brick, stone, and concrete; that's many a city sidewalk. In addition to the signature wellness benefit of grounding, *pluggz* were biomechanically engineered for genuine comfort and fashionably styled.

Pluggz commissioned a study to see if our shoes stepped up to our expectations and to prove the efficacy of our plug as a grounding technology. In our placebo-controlled single-blind pilot study, subjects were assessed after baseline measures were taken on the physiological changes that were produced by wearing *pluggz* shoes for a period of ten minutes. Using Gas Discharge Visualization devices, Thought Technology ProComp, Physiology Suite with BioGraph Infiniti, and CardioPro software, significant changes in heart, head, thyroid, adrenal, and lumber responses were detected. Taken as a whole these changes are indicative of the body's relaxation response.

"The data shows the early markers of the onset of a relaxation response," said Melinda Connor, PhD, who is the chief investigator at Optimal Healing Research, the independent researching firm retained to oversee the study. "In addition, the increase in spectral brightness in the fingers and hands indicate improved electro-dermal skin response"—probably due to an increase in circulation.

Connor added that findings from this pilot were particularly significant because the subjects were tested for only ten minutes on parched desert ground that had no moisture.

With these findings underfoot, Sharon created the *pluggz* motto: Change your shoes, change your life.

CHAPTER THIRTEEN

Mother Nature and Earth
MOTHERS

Nurturers by nature, mothers are givers of life, which is why, in the simplest terms, the Earth has been given this feminine attribute. That the Earth is also the greatest healer of all time, providing everything that's needed to sustain and maintain every living thing, makes the image of parental nurturer even more apropos.

The mother of two, Dr. Laura Koniver is also a healer. Schooled in traditional medicine before changing her professional focus and hanging up her office-issued stethoscope, she hung up her shingle as an Intuition Physician a decade ago, a move she credits to motherhood and Mother Nature.

She was practicing traditional medicine while she was pregnant with her first child, taking time off from work shortly after her daughter was born. But after returning to work, she had an epiphany about the way modern medicine is practiced.

"Here I was rushing patients in and out of the examining room, not taking the time to make any meaningful connection with them, and just spending enough time to evaluate their symptoms and send them home with a prescription, when it hit me on a stomach-wrenching, heart-hurting level," she said. "These people came to me for their care, putting their trust and health in my hands, and I was treating them as a number or a statistic or a symptom or a prescription for pills. It sickened me on a deep level to finally realize that each person on Earth is as precious and valuable as my very own children, but then to just treat them medically on the surface was not right."

"Medical school," she explained, "teaches you how to evaluate and treat an illness, but it does not teach you how to connect to a patient on an intuitive and meaningful soul-level, which is essential in the healing process." She discovered that motherhood teaches all that and more.

"Becoming a mother completely dissolved my notions of what I should be doing and the career I had worked so hard to achieve. It opened me up and took me out of the equation. It no longer mattered what degree I had earned and what I was thinking and if I was scholarly. It only mattered that I hold a space for this precious amazing soul of my daughter. All I had to do was hold her and breathe and I felt complete."

Laura happily stayed home with her daughter, and soon a son, while they were young, tending to their well-being in ways she had hoped to do as a practicing doctor. One of those ways was grounding.

"As a baby, my daughter suffered from colic. It affected her eating habits, her moods, and her sleep," shared Laura. "I used to gather her up, skin-to-skin, and go outside for a walk to try to calm her down. We lived in Arizona then so I was usually barefoot all the time."

Laura found that every time she would take a walk, baby in tow, the crying would stop and her little one would fall asleep, pain free. But invariably as soon as they returned inside, the pain and the tears returned, too.

It wasn't the sound of the birds, the wind rustling in the trees, or the fresh air outside that had this soothing affect on Laura's baby. "When we would go out for a drive in the car, windows open, nature's noises all around us, she would still cry," said Laura, who realized, without knowing the specifics of grounding as medicine, that the barefoot walks had everything to do with making her baby feel better.

Once she made the connection, she started to do the research, reading everything she could about natural healing and the Earth, discovering it to be a truly universal restorative modality. She also made sure that she took her baby out for a walk at least three times a day, knowing that she would fall asleep and rest peacefully during those times. "It was survival for both of us," Laura said.

Later when her son was born, she made sure that both kids spent time outdoors every day, playing in mud puddles, running barefoot in the grass, getting dirty like children did not too long ago. We mentioned earlier that insulating children from the ground like we do now has led to dire consequences on their health. Laura knew this instinctively.

As her children grew, Laura took up painting, thinking that she might earn a living as an artist. Anxious, she met with a friend, an energy healer by vocation, and asked her advice. Laura still remembers what her friend said. We're paraphrasing here but basically it was about the importance of getting grounded before you do anything in life. Take a breath, feel the energy in your body down to your root chakra, breathe again. Get grounded. The concept of getting grounded resonated with Laura and it helped her make her next move.

She began to paint chakras—energy focal points, bodily functions or psychic node in the subtle body—brilliant in color and intuitive in nature, eventually using them as healing tools when she later welcomed patients back into her life. They come to her now both for her medical expertise, compassionately dispensed, but also for her knowledge about the healing nature of Earth.

"I have learned that it is abnormal for a body to be ungrounded," she said. "We need to get our natural connection back with the Earth if we are to be truly in a state of optimal well-being."

As she explains it, grounding is key for so many wellness issues, from her firsthand knowledge of using it to treat her children's painful colic and her son's seasonal allergies to the oft-diagnosed ADHD (attention deficit hyperactivity disorder) and autism spectrum diseases many children suffer with today.

Why? Because in addition to its inflammation fighting abilities, grounding helps people get the sleep they need for their health. A continual lack of sleep prevents a person's body and mind from getting restored and recharged. Those recommended

eight hours of sleep are not prescribed lightly because nighttime, set by nature thousands of years ago, is purposely reserved for rest and remedy.

Grounding, as the studies show, helps regulate the body's natural cortisol level, allowing a person to fall asleep and stay asleep naturally. Sleeping grounded is key to people's health, especially children whose bodies and minds are growing every day. There's a domino effect on children who are sleep deprived, including decreased appetite, lack of focus, and behavior problems. Doctors often prescribe medication to help youngsters sleep. Laura says all that is needed is grounding.

Parents often tell her that their children are outside all of the time, playing sports, enjoying recess, and otherwise spending time in the great outdoors. Isn't that enough to maintain their contact with the Earth? She explains that the shoes and uniforms they wear and the tarred paved areas they play on do not allow grounding.

"Everyone in my family sleeps grounded," she said, explaining that she puts grounding pads on all their beds. She also keeps grounding mats near their computers, so that they can rest their hand or feet on them while they are playing their video games or doing their homework. She also wears shoes that are grounding and advises her patients to do the same.

Says Laura, "We have exhaustively looked at the human body while it is grounded indoors—many times while directly hooked up to electrical devices in a sleep study lab, or with EEG monitors on the brain, and certainly always surrounded by EMFs and using office and home wiring for the grounding tool—and still the body heals.

Blood viscosity decreases. Blood pressure normalizes. Brain wave patterns relax. Muscle tension decreases. Pain lifts. Mood lightens. Over time, hormones normalize. Cortisol drops. Blood sugars stabilize. Sleep deepens. Inflammation decreases. The human body heals.

"I believe we are at a crossroads where grounding our body is not only a smart healing practice to develop, but it's actually mandatory if we want to experience healing in modern society."

To reap the benefits of grounding you don't have to lie down with your entire body touching the ground. "The beauty of grounding is that even if just one tiny cell is grounded, then your whole body is grounded," she said.

Each cell and bone in our bodies is naturally conductive and connected to one another by an interwoven gel-like plasma network. Contact with one cell connects it to all the other cells, bones, joints, and organs in your body. And the benefits of grounding are immediate and not on a time-delay as other medical treatments are.

"Once you disconnect your body from the Earth's energy source, you'll stop being actively grounded," she said, adding that there is a cumulative effect to regular grounding.

Nature made us resilient. Even though many of us are suffering from the effects of not living grounded, once we do get back in touch with Mother Earth, we start to take back our health, too. Which is exactly what mothers have wanted for their families since the beginning of time.

CHAPTER FOURTEEN

Feet on the
GROUND

YOGA
CONNECTIONS

Yoga, rooted in ancient Indian traditions that date back more than 5,000 years, has gained a strong foothold in modern-day America, not just for its physical fitness and stress relief attributes, but also as a healthy lifestyle choice that has stood the test of time. A survey conducted by *Yoga Alliance and Yoga Journal*[1] reports that the number of Americans doing yoga has grown by over fifty percent in the last four years to over 36 million as of 2016, up from 20.4 million in 2012. While the majority of yoga practitioners are women (seventy-two percent), the number of American men doing yoga has more than doubled, going from 4 million in 2012 to 10 million in 2016. The number of American adults over fifty doing yoga has tripled over the last four years to reach 14 million. And eighty one percent of practitioners have practiced yoga outside of the studio in the last twelve months. It is reported to be a $27 billion industry today.

Going back to the days of David Thoreau, poet, philosopher, transcendentalist, and nature lover, was considered by many to be the first self-described yogi in America. His two years living on Walden Pond, practicing yoga, grounding too, even though the term had not yet been defined, and writing about it has inspired and informed the work of naturalists, environmentalists, and writers, for the past 150 years. His neighbors thought him to be a bit off, a misanthropic hermit, whose habit of sitting cross-legged in the open doorway of his cabin for hours on end, losing himself in nature left them leery about his state of mind. Of his daily morning ritual, Thoreau penned, "This was not time subtracted from my life, but so much over and above my usual allowance."

That's part of the appeal of both yoga and grounding, two practices that are uniquely healing and life enriching on many levels. Across the board, people believe that yoga is good for you. Medical studies back them up with findings that confirm that yoga can help improve cardiovascular fitness, flexibility, balance, and overall quality of life. Plus it reduces stress, anxiety, and pain like grounding does.

While contemporary Western yoga typically focuses on stress-relieving physical poses with lots of stretching and bending, yoga, in its purest form, includes a rich history of philosophical and ethical principles, breathing exercises, and meditation.

Even within the physical practice, yoga guides practitioners to connect the movement of their body and the fluctuations of the mind to the rhythm of their breath. This connection between the mind, body, and breath helps direct attention inward as people become more aware of what they are experiencing from moment to moment. That awareness is what makes yoga a practice, rather than a task or a goal to be completed.

MOUNTAIN POSE TEACHES US, LITERALLY, HOW TO STAND ON
OUR OWN TWO FEET . . . TEACHING US TO ROOT OURSELVES
INTO THE EARTH . . . . OUR BODIES BECOME A CONNECTION
BETWEEN HEAVEN AND EARTH.
—*Carol Krucoff*

The building blocks of yoga are poses. You may be familiar with the downward-facing dog pose, great for anyone who suffers from back pain and one of the most grounding yoga poses where both hands and feet are planted squarely on the ground, or the tree pose, good for your posture and balance and probably one of the most recognizable of the yoga poses. Standing poses like the tree, mountain, and warrior teach you how to connect to the Earth and draw energy up through your feet and legs into the rest of your body. In the mountain pose, you simply stand straight up with feet slightly apart and eyes closed and focus on feeling "grounded." Your teacher might encourage you to really "ground down" and grow from there.

In the tree pose, you stand on one leg with the other one bent at the knee with your foot place on the inner thigh in a half lotus position. Keeping calm and focused while balancing on one foot will teach you to sway gently like a tree in the wind, steady and sure no matter what the outside circumstances may be. Trees are one of the most powerfully grounded things on this planet with much of the tree rooted beneath the surface. Think about how many trees survive powerful winds and are not uprooted year after year. That's because they are so grounded in the Earth. That image alone is much like the visualizations used in yoga. When you are in tree pose, you may visualize your feet rooted in the Earth as the tree's roots are. You learn to stay grounded while maintaining the ability to sway at the same time. What an important life tool for those times when you need to stay balanced and steady in the face of adversity. The three warrior poses, all of them powerfully grounding, help you gain inner strength and courage, letting you open up to yourself and others.

PRACTICE IN NATURE. TOUCH THE GROUND AND SENSE
SOMETHING BEAUTIFUL. THAT MICROCOSM OF THE UNIVERSE
CONNECTS YOU TO YOUR OWN TRUE NATURE.
—*Amy Weintraub*

Amy Weintraub, author and founder of LifeForce Yoga®, a program that integrates and synthesizes a range of ancient and evidence-based, adaptive yoga practices that go beyond the physical to incorporate mood management and trauma recovery into whatever yoga style or lineage a person wishes to study. Her motivation was personal, coming about as she was on a healing quest to overcome depression, trauma, and the mind-numbing medications that often accompany a person's downslide. She found healing and strength through yoga, and the inherent state of calm and grounding it promises. She has since made it her mission to share it with others who have experienced trauma in their lives through compassionate self-awareness. "When they learn to channel bliss states through yoga, they do so by grounding techniques."

Amy integrates energizing sounds she developed, based on ancient mantras called *bijas*, to work through trauma and manage mood. She teaches pulsing lums and vums and motivating mantras for strength or courage or peace. In her personal practice, she begins outside at the beach or in the mountains whenever she can. Sunrise is her favorite time of the day, a time when she greets the sun and connects to the universe and nature.

Silicon Valley entrepreneur Dave Asprey, best-selling author whose books include *The Bulletproof Diet* and *Head Strong: The Bulletproof Plan to Activate Untapped Brain Energy* and founder of Bulletproof, the world's first human performance and nutrition company, has a busy schedule traveling all over the world talking about his wellness regimen. To combat jet lag, he regularly practices grounding. He did it the first time quite by accident, and it turned out to be an intuitive move on his part, when he took his morning yoga routine outside in the park by his hotel, to reset his energy. He knew that raising body temperature by exercising in the morning was effective for resetting circadian rhythms. What he didn't know at the time was that grounding was also key to putting one's body back in balance. He remembers feeling how doing yoga that particular morning made all the difference in the way he felt. "It was incredible. I did not experience the negative effects of jet lag at all." Thinking at first that it was the early morning yoga that reenergized him, he tried yoga indoors on the next trip, doing the same exercises at the same time of day. To no avail, he admitted. But when he took his yoga back outside, it dawned on him that it was the act of grounding itself that made him feel so refreshed. He admits that for a long time he kept his newfound discovery to himself, but now touts grounding as one of his secret tools for being Bulletproof.

IT'S NOT WHAT YOU LOOK AT THAT MATTERS. IT'S WHAT YOU SEE.
—*Henry David Thoreau*

Pay attention to your surroundings with all of your five senses. Then lay down on the Earth to unwind and reset. When it is time to leave, bring your body in to the child's resting pose, your head touching the Earth, your heart filled with gratitude.

I WENT TO THE WOODS BECAUSE I WISHED TO LIVE
DELIBERATELY, TO FRONT ONLY THE ESSENTIAL FACTS OF LIFE,
AND SEE IF I COULD NOT LEARN WHAT IT HAD TO TEACH, AND
NOT, WHEN I CAME TO DIE, DISCOVER THAT I HAD NOT LIVED.
—*Henry David Thoreau*

CHAPTER FIFTEEN

Ancient Movement Arts and
GROUNDING

We sat down with Michael Gelb, Brain Trust Charity's Brain of the Year award winner, fourteen-time author, teacher, sought-after motivational speaker, and the preeminent authority on creative genius and leadership. His best-selling books about creativity and innovation, including *How to Think Like Leonardo Da Vinci: Seven Steps to Genius Every Day,* and *Brain Power: Improve Your Mind as You Age,* have inspired generations of big thinkers and doers. At the core of his curriculum is mindfulness, and at its core, grounding.

"I have been practicing Tai Chi and Aikido martial arts for decades," he said, saying that he never fails to feel the energy and connection with the ground. "The Earth, after all, is where everything starts."

Michael, a dedicated student of methodologies for self-awareness, trained as a teacher of the Alexander technique and turned his master's thesis on the subject into his first book, *Body Learning: An Introduction to the Alexander Technique,* still selling strong more than thirty years after its first publication.

The Alexander Technique is a body-oriented practice that changes the way a person thinks and responds in everyday activities, ultimately improving ease and freedom of movement, balance, support, and coordination. The technique, according to people who have studied this method, puts them on a path that enhances their comfort and increases their pleasure in all their activities, leaving them feeling lighter, freer, and more grounded.

IN TODAY'S RUSH, WE ALL THINK TOO MUCH—SEEK TOO MUCH—
WANT TOO MUCH—AND FORGET ABOUT THE JOY OF JUST BEING.
—*Eckhart Tolle*

Michael Gelb's immersion into this technique laid the foundation for a life that is balanced with poise, performance, and a passion for meaningful connections. When he's not out on the road inspiring his global audiences with his insights and expertise, he makes time for his daily hour-long walks along the wooded trails of the Rockefeller State Preserve abutting his property, practicing Tai Chi and Qigong to recharge and realign with nature's grounding essence. "I like to feel the ground when I am outside; its energy is palpable."

He shared a story about a consulting assignment he was on in Wilmington, Delaware, at a Dow Chemical plant. Michael was tasked with teaching a team of chemical engineers the art of creative thinking. Their environment was the antithesis of an idea-generating think tank. They worked in a cement building in rows of uniform cubicles where they interacted with computer screens all day to get their work done.

"I had them all take a twenty-minute walk around the building for their midday break. The setting was beautiful, with nature and trees all around," said Michael. "They felt more relaxed and creative after their walks and it showed in their work. It's a simple thing to do for your health and productivity but people don't think of doing it."

MINDFULNESS ISN'T DIFFICULT. WE JUST NEED TO REMEMBER TO DO IT.
—*Sharon Salzberg*

That's what mindfulness does, it makes you think about where you are and what you're doing, and it's interesting to note how it so often manifests from a walk in nature.

"You shouldn't have to write this book," he said at the end of our conversation. "We shouldn't have to show people how to reconnect with our sense of naturalness, how to benefit from the natural flow of support and balance that's always there for us. It's something we all should know and do naturally. We should be like the trees and not have to do anything at all to be grounded. Trees stand in harmony with the Earth. They are not stressed or miserable. They are happy.

"People, on the other hand," he continued, "are out of alignment, depressed, and distressed. As humans, we spend too much time in synthetic environments, disconnected from the outside world. We take drugs to try to achieve that natural state of balance in our lives instead of turning to the greatest pharmacy that's available to us right at our feet."

When you are grounded, you are very much like that strong tree. You're present in your body and connected to the Earth. You're not as vulnerable or thrown off course as that leaf that's blown around every which way when the wind blows. You feel centered and balanced no matter what is going on around you.

"Nature brings your attention into the moment. It's common sense to start with the ground to feel the support that's available to you. However you make the connection is fine," advised Michael, whether its through sports, walking, dancing, gardening, or a mindful practice. He started with Aikido, the martial arts technique he saw on the Kung Fu shows of his youth. Loosely translated, Aikido is described as "a way of unifying (with) life energy" or as "the way of harmonious spirit." Michael found it to be powerful, graceful, and harmonious all at once, not to mention incredibly cool.

As his lifestyle changed, he moved on to age-old practices like Tai Chi and Qigong, both of which cultivate the Qi, the life energy that flows through the body's energy pathways. That's what he does now, mindfully reconnecting to the Earth as he travels across the globe sharing indispensable insights about things our ancestors naturally knew.

Dr. Christy Garner, an expert in the field of epigenetics and a wellness advocate who is committed to finding the simplest tools that make the biggest difference for people in achieving health and happiness, is a huge proponent of grounding as a treatment for mood and anxiety disorders. Her specialty is helping children and adults with highly sensitive nervous systems cope and control their challenges. These include autism, ADHD, anxiety, hair pulling, skin picking, obsessive compulsive-disorder (OCD), seizures, head banging, and addiction. Over the last decade, she has worked with over 2,400 individuals with highly sensitive nervous systems, drawing from her clinical knowledge and training, along with her personal experience and real-life navigation of living with anxiety disorders.

What works best in support of the nervous system and health? "Reconnecting," she says emphatically. "Reconnecting with our innate ability to heal, to each other, and to the limitless healing power of the Earth." She has found that traditional ground to body practices like yoga, Tai Chi, and simply touching the Earth while walking, sitting, or running barefoot, has the power to maintain vibrant health and stabilize the nervous system almost immediately. Children really benefit from grounding, not only for the electron transfer that takes place to equalize the body's energy, but also because connecting to the Earth keeps them in their bodies she explains.

"I can attest to the power of grounding on nervous system disorders not just as a practitioner, but as someone who personally suffered from anxiety from the age of nine to thirty-three. I had tried everything I could to stem my anxiety issues and emotional behaviors, from cleaning up my diet to taking medicine and more. Nothing helped until I heard about grounding. Grounding has the ability to make individuals with highly stimulated nervous systems more resilient, and less susceptible to outside distractions. It enables people to handle things that might otherwise throw them off course and it keeps them rooted in the body.

"I spend my days and nights grounded and it has made all the difference. And the people I counsel in my practice? I make it a point to give them all the tools and tips they need to stay grounded. It is such an easy fix and one that everyone can take advantage of."

Jason Wachob, author of *Wellth: How I Learned to Build a Life, Not a Résumé*, and founder and CEO of mindbodygreen.com, talks a lot about grounding in his book, and advocates that exercising outdoors, in nature, is most beneficial. In fact, ground is one of his ten "verbs" for building and living a balanced life. He writes that, "Grounding, the process of walking barefoot and sinking your feet into the sand or ground, is an awesome healing practice! Connecting with the Earth's electrons has some awesome physiological benefits! I'd never thought I'd say that as a native New Yorker!"

We're glad he did.

QUIET THE MIND, AND THE SOUL WILL SPEAK.
—*Ma Jaya Sati Bhagavati*

Meditation, archaeologists and scholars agree, has been around for 5,000 years, starting first in the Far East and spreading to Western society thousands of years later. It gained popularity in the US in the 1960s and '70s, but it was not until recently that the medical profession began to test the effects of meditation on a person's health, especially as a relaxation-focused antidote to stress.

A study by Harvard University and the University of Sienna[1] found that the powers of meditation move beyond the cultivation of self-awareness, improvement of concentration, and protection of the heart and immune system—it can actually alter the physiology of the human brain. Consistent practice can help alleviate symptoms of anxiety and depression in people who need it most. Imagine taking your meditation practice outside, where the healing power of the Earth's energy enhances the proven powerful possibilities of the body/mind connection.

No matter how prevalent and popular in our multicultural society, many of us still associate meditation with Buddhism, visualizing the rotund ever-smiling deity sitting lotus-style under a tree, his temple of nature. That smile he wears? Some say the secret of the Buddha's smile lies in the mastery of his mind—through the practice of meditation. We might add that meditating under a tree also has something to do with it.

The natural world was ever-present in the Buddha's life and teachings. Those who listened to his teachings did so sitting on the ground among the trees. For centuries, many Buddhists not only found it helpful to practice outdoors in natural settings, they felt the underlying support and protection that's inherent in the Earth as they embraced their meditation. A long tradition in Buddhism sees an intimate and mutual interaction between nature and people's inner life; the health of the natural environment is closely tied to people's physical and spiritual health. Caring for the environment is a way to care for ourselves. It's no surprise that monasteries and meditation centers are often located in a forested or jungle setting for few things support the opening of the heart and mind like the beauty and tranquility of the natural world.

People who meditate in nature, grounded, find it easier to fully embrace and embody the senses, which in turn creates a deep sense of calm. They find that they are much more awake and alert, more open, and relaxed. Contemplation becomes more accessible and effortless in the outdoors, they say, suggesting that they become less concerned with their endless thoughts and drama and instead are drawn to the heightened sensitivity of the present. So palpable are their experiences when they reconnect to nature, they say they actually feel their stress melt into the ground.

We were inspired by members of the TED Talk community who shared what they do to find time for stillness and reflection. Among their answers, curator Chris Anderson said, "Water, pine trees, cliffs, meadows . . . doesn't matter. All nature will do. Walk a little, dream a little." Brené Brown, who talks about vulnerability, goes swimming. "It's exercise, meditation, and therapy in one." Stress expert Kelly McGonigal practices yoga and meditation, but she also likes to get up early in the morning and go out for a walk. We are more affected by our landscape than we might imagine. Anytime you can go outside of the box and expose yourself to the healing influence of nature you should take that opportunity. We'll be right there with you.

CHAPTER SIXTEEN

Take a Walk on the
WILD SIDE

The history of nature cures began in the dawn of human history when cavemen sought relief from their maladies in their own backyards and indigenous natives looked for healing remedies to treat themselves and members of their tribal community. Their teachers? The wildlife that shared the landscapes where they lived. The animals' plant-eating, ground-pawing, and water-splashing behavior caught their attention. They took note that their wild brethren would often eat certain leaves, roots, plants, and minerals when they appeared a bit off and acted differently from the rest of the herd.

Their early observations led to practices that formed the basis of most healing practices, for thousands of years the only curative means available to humanity. American Indians watched wild bears dig up and use the roots of Ligusticum plants so often they named the plant "bear medicine." Other examples manifest in catnip, hare's lettuce, pigweed, and horny-goat weed. No explanations needed. Growing scientific evidence today backs up the premise that wildlife uses nature as healer, both for the medicinal properties of the plant life they eat but also for the power of the Earth itself to aid in their healing.

Steve Kroschel shares his Alaskan homestead with a host of two- and four-footed furred and feathered friends, including Karen the orphan moose. In all cases, Steve has been able to closely observe how the animals and birds interact with nature. And in turn, he welcomes visitors to his home to "teach people about the Earth through animals." Karen came to live with Steve as a baby moose. She demonstrated her preference for sleeping grounded early on in a blind test by purposely choosing a grounding pad as her bed of choice in an otherwise ungrounded trailer. Turns out when she couldn't feel the Earth beneath her feet, she naturally gravitated to the next best thing.

CLEARLY, ANIMALS KNOW MORE THAN WE THINK, AND THINK A
GREAT DEAL MORE THAN WE KNOW.
—*Irene M. Pepperberg*

Without the services of a veterinarian nearby, wild animals seem to know best when it comes to their health, actively helping themselves to stay well. Scientists and researchers have documented a number of cases where animals sought out their own medicinal protocols for a variety of treatable ailments. And there's a term for it now. It's called zoopharmacognosy.

They observed capuchin monkeys that rub their fur with millipedes containing insect-killing chemicals called benzoquinones; chimpanzees who eat the pith of the plant Vernonia amygdalina to kill off intestinal worms; gorillas that eat clay to absorb toxins and pathogens; and elephants that make pilgrimages to a cave complex to dig out the soft rock in the cave walls, grind, and then swallow it for added protection against toxins they may ingest from eating plants.

EVERY ANIMAL KNOWS MORE THAN YOU DO.
—*Nez Perce*

Does your dog or cat eat grass only to throw up afterwards? This is a healthy response to sickness that emanates from their wild ancestors. Denied such material today say the experts, a cat will attack houseplants or chew wool sweaters. Dogs might also be doctoring themselves when they eat or lick sand, soil, rocks, and clay or chew on your socks if nothing natural is available to help them vomit what ails them.

Have you ever seen a dog walk in a tight circle and twirl before settling down in his bed? In the wild, animals do that too, tamping down their spot and digging down in the cool Earth to regulate their temperature for the night ahead and recharge their energy for the next day.

That animals in the wild sleep grounded in caves, in the woods, in the trees, or in the bush is a given. But when they are injured or hurt, they dig holes in the Earth or lay down in the grass to help heal their wounds naturally, letting the anti-inflammatory grounding properties go to work. A sick animal retires to a secluded place and fasts until it feels better. Sick elephants are known to separate from the herd and remain near shade and water. Hedgehogs, normally nocturnal, will sit in the sun on the open ground when they're feeling under the weather. Even cows will lie down in the pasture aligning themselves with the Earth's magnetic fields according to some studies that also noted that deer, turtles, and birds also have this propensity for naturally grounding outside.

Did you know that many pets manifest the same diseases as their owners? Scientists say this phenomenon is clearly caused by environment. Wild animals don't exhibit the inflammation and stress-related conditions that indoor pets and zoo animals do. Nor are they as sedentary as cats and dogs that are kept inside.

So how can we make sure our indoor pets experience the healing benefits their wild counterparts enjoy? Taking them for daily walks on an unpaved surface is the easiest, of course, letting them run in the grass, on a wooded trail or sandy beach for optimal grounding benefits. Let them stay outside thirty minutes or an hour if you can. While you are helping them, you're also helping yourself. A study at the University of Missouri showed that walking the dog was actually more effective for weight loss than having a membership in a gym or joining a diet plan.[1]

Studies have shown that animals naturally gravitate to grounded surfaces. Animals have a kind of sixth sense that lets them detect changes in barometric pressure and electromagnetic discharges even before storms surface. Animals can sense impending danger by detecting subtle or abrupt shifts in the environment. Earthquakes bring vibrational changes on land and in water while storms cause electromagnetic changes in the atmosphere. Our pets have been noticed to do the same, and in the case of integrative wellness veterinarian, Dr. Karen Becker, her cats and dogs vie for a spot on her grounding pads when lightening strikes in the skies outside her home.

Own a plant instead of a pet? Make sure it's grounded too. Several scientific and curious plant owners have tested the theory that plants and flowers respond to grounding, documenting earlier seed sprouting and explosive growth in potted plants to longer vase life for cut flowers.

One study by electrical engineer T. Galen Hieronymus (1895–1988)[2] grew plants in complete darkness in his basement by grounding the tops of the boxes with a copper wire that was connected to a series of metal plates that were positioned outside the house in places of direct sunlight. According to Hieronymus, vibrant green plants sprouted despite the absence of sunlight.

Gary E. Schwartz, PhD, professor of psychology, medicine, neurology, psychiatry, and surgery in the University of Arizona's Health Sciences Department, performed a double-blind proof-of-concept study grounding cut sunflowers.[3] He found that the grounded sunflowers lived for an additional ten days longer than the sunflowers that were not connected to the Earth. The grounded vase's water remained as clean and clear as the first day he filled the vases. Steve Kroschel and others did similar tests, and shared similar findings.

Our conclusion? Every living thing on our planet, furred, feathered, finned, two- and four-footed, flowered, leaf-covered, and rooted, thrives stronger and longer by direct daily contact with the Earth.

CHAPTER SEVENTEEN

Walking into the **Future:** Prescription
"VITAMIN GROUND"

THE DOCTOR OF THE FUTURE WILL GIVE
NO MEDICINE BUT WILL INTEREST HIS PATIENTS IN THE CARE
OF THE HUMAN FRAME, IN DIET, AND IN THE CAUSE AND
PREVENTION OF DISEASE.
—*Thomas Edison*

While the practice of alternative medicine has been around for thousands of years, for decades its modern day proponents have been viewed with skepticism, if not downright dismissed as laughable and on the fringe. As a result, contemporary practitioners—microbiologists, behavioral scientists, researchers, and physicians among them—who unilaterally believe in the healing power of body, mind, and spirit therapies have been fighting an uphill battle to be taken seriously by their conservative scientific and medical counterparts who doubt the efficacy of these practices in the wellness arena.

Natural healers are a tenacious and passionate group. Fortunately for us, these practitioners persisted and paved a path that has had tremendous impact on our understanding of health and medicine. Their teachings and findings have opened doors—and minds—to the possibilities of age-old healing philosophies, mainstreaming ancient practices like yoga, meditation, energy healing, and Tai Chi, and resurrecting gems of ancient wisdoms like grounding.

"The interesting thing is that the health impact of these practices, which have been part of global cultures for thousands of years, were mapped out long ago by the sages who had discovered and shared them," said psychologist and scientist Dr. Shamini Jain. She is the founder and director of the Consciousness and Healing Initiative and a pioneer in the newly defined area of biofield medicine, based on the theory that our body's own energy field "regulates everything from our cellular function to our nervous system."

"While the west has been slower to adapt and adopt these practices as an integral part of an overall wellness plan, new scientific research that examines us as the agents of change for our own healing would help to herald a true shift in the practice of medicine."

THE ART OF HEALING COMES FROM NATURE AND NOT FROM
THE PHYSICIAN. THEREFORE, THE PHYSICIAN MUST START FROM
NATURE WITH AN OPEN MIND.
—*Paracelsus*

"As more and more of us take charge of our health through integrative body, mind, and spirit practices, we have an opportunity to shape the new paradigm in health and medicine. We can choose to watch as industry dollars utilize scientific advances to advance the next wave of Big Pharma, or we can choose to support research that will irrefutably map the impact of nature and our consciousness on our own health, so that we can better directly heal ourselves and prevent disease before it starts. We must choose to support the research and education that will truly empower our own health and healing, to usher in the real future of medicine," advises Shamini.

While industry may look for man-made healing solutions, we have seen that the future of medicine is deeply rooted in the past and grounded in nature. We also talked about this with Shamini who passionately shared her professional and personal expertise on healing now and for the future.

"For too long western medicine has followed the mantra that healing is simply the absence of disease. If we get rid of the disease, we are healed," she said. But her beliefs hold, like ours, that healing results in a harmony of mind, emotion, body, and the environment. They are all interconnected and together enable the body to heal itself.

THE ART OF MEDICINE CONSISTS IN AMUSING THE PATIENT
WHILE NATURE CURES THE DISEASE.
—*Voltaire*

Thanks to the efforts of Shamani and others, biofield medicine is making strides on the healing front and grounding is one of its most promising agents. "When you're connecting with energy of the Earth, you are grounding yourself with life's energy from the ground up. Not only is grounding essential for preventing burn out, it puts your body back to its naturally balanced state by connecting to your natural frequency and getting some electrical nutrition." In fact, research shows the Earth's frequency is the same as our natural frequency (bio field) as well as that of animals.

That grounding has remained on a solid footing for its natural healing abilities since man first walked the Earth bodes well for the health of mankind now and in the future. Perhaps we will soon find it the norm to go directly to the Earth for a remedy instead of running to the doctor for another new pill.

As Jurriaan Kamp, solutions-oriented editor of *The Intelligent Optimist*, says, "Grounding makes absolute sense." Jurriaan has spent more than twenty-five years looking for solutions for all sorts of challenges, including finding workable protocols for health and happiness. Does he think they'll be found in more clever pills? He doesn't believe that. Does he think that hospitals are the best places to heal? For some things he says yes, like a broken leg that needs to be set, a surgical procedure that needs to be done, or a major infection that needs an immediate regimen of antibiotics.

Jurriaan reminds us that eighty percent of the illnesses that plague our American population are caused by autoimmune and chronic diseases. "Western medicine can find and treat the symptoms, but it is not getting to the cause. Alternative health treatments or integrative whole body therapies have a far bigger chance to succeed in healing us. We know our body's energy system is more complex than our physical bodies and that health and well-being is more about the metaphysical than just moving our blood cells around."

He recalled when a friend of his was diagnosed with breast cancer and went to the hospital for surgery. She opted out of anesthesia and instead chose to undergo acupuncture as her sedative of choice. That was more than twenty years ago. Today, acupuncture is commonly available for use in trauma surgery in hospital emergency rooms throughout the nation.

Imagine how far we've come in terms of our knowledge and use of age-old practices that the Chinese performed for thousands of years. They came up with simple solutions for health maladies that people had beneficial experiences with. Many modern-day medicine men cite the placebo effect when mind, body, spirit therapies have positive outcomes. But the mind is a strong healer too, and it holds great promise as we find answers to our most pressing health concerns.

The Ancients knew. What is old is now fast becoming new. For both of us, getting grounded and practicing grounding every day has changed us, enhancing our health and well-being in myriad—and ultimately priceless—ways.

It wasn't that long ago when the medical community acknowledged the inherent health dangers of vitamin D deficiency, a condition all too prevalent due to our indoor lifestyles and sunscreened bodies. Now, because of the very real concerns that a lack of vitamin D has on our health, it is well known today. In that same vein, we are advocating that the ill effects of grounding deficiency or *vitamin ground*, is becoming mainstream, too. We think it merits the same, if not more, consideration and concern that vitamin D deficiency has garnered with the medical community and the general public.

A CHANGING ENVIRONMENT AND A CHANGING WORLD

Clearly health care and the field of medicine are in transition. Conventional treatments are giving way to an expanded, integrative medical model that is now incorporating the old with the new, and the high-tech with the all-natural as we all strive to find cures for chronic diseases and pain. We believe grounding is integral to this movement. The by-product of our fast-paced evolving society is that we have come indoors, moved away from the Earth, headed up into high rises, and shielded our feet with synthetic soled shoes. As a result, we've become disconnected and unnaturally insulated from the continuous flow of Earth's natural and beneficial energy.

> MAN MUST CEASE ATTRIBUTING HIS PROBLEMS TO HIS
> ENVIRONMENT, AND LEARN AGAIN TO EXERCISE HIS WILL—
> HIS PERSONAL RESPONSIBILITY.
> —*Albert Einstein*

The world is focused now, and rightly so, on environmental sustainability. But we also need to focus on what we regard as human sustainability and well-being through grounding. In this book, we've shared the research, stories, and reasons for reconnecting with the Earth. We've documented the whys and ways for everyone of every age, ability, and address to take advantage of the most sustainable and freely accessible health resource there is, the Earth. Along with the pioneers, people, practitioners—and pets—cited in this book, we've both integrated grounding into our daily lives and we know it works. We hope you will take the steps to get grounded in good health too.

Please let us know how grounding works for you. We would love to hear from you at stories@barefootwisdom.com.

OUR PRESCRIPTION
FOR YOUR FUTURE

Finally, we want to leave you with our last inspiration. Imagine if your primary care practitioner gave you a prescription with just two words on it: "Get Grounded."

We imagine it would look something like this.

R̶X̶ for HEALTH

PRESCRIPTION

Name: *You*

Rx: *Get Grounded.*

Dose: *Daily, as many times a day as you can*

Contraindications: *None*

Refills: *Unlimited*

Cost: *Priceless*

Signature: *Mother Earth*

WE ENCOURAGE YOU TO GIVE IT A TRY.

ENDNOTES

CHAPTER FOUR

1. Daniel T. C. Cox, Danielle F. Shanahan, Hannah L. Hudson, Richard A. Fuller, Karen Anderson, Steven Hancock, and Kevin J. Gaston, "Doses of Nearby Nature Simultaneously Associated with Multiple Health Benefits," *Journal of Affective Disorders*, 2013. *Int J Environ Res Public Health*. 2017 Feb; 14(2): 172. Published online 2017 Feb 9. doi: 10.3390/ijerph14020172.

2. Marc G. Berman, Ethan Kross, Katherine M. Krpan, Mary K. Askren, Aleah Burson, Patricia J. Deldin, Stephen Kaplan, Lindsey Sherdell, Ian H. Gotlib, and John Jonides, "Interacting with Nature Improves Cognition and Affect for Individuals with Depression," *Psychological Science, 2012*. Published in final edited form as: *J Affect Disord*. 2012 Nov; 140(3): 300–305. Published online 2012 Mar 31. doi: 10.1016/j.jad.2012.03.012.

3. Melissa R. Marselle, Katherine N. Irvine, and Sara L. Warber, "Walking for Well-Being: Are Group Walks in Certain Types of Natural Environments Better for Well-Being Than Group Walks in Urban Environments?" *Psychological Science, 2008. Int J Environ Res Public Health*. 2013 Nov; 10(11): 5603–5628. Published online 2013 Oct 29. doi: 10.3390/ijerph10115603.

4. Gregory N. Bratman, J. Paul Hamilton, Kevin S. Hahn, Gretchen C. Daily, and James J. Gross, "Nature Experience Reduces Rumination and Subgenual Prefrontal Cortex Activation," *Proceedings of the National Academy of Sciences*, 2011, 2015.

5. Marily Oppezzo and Daniel Schwartz, "Give Your Ideas Some Legs: The Positive Effect of Walking on Creative Thinking," *Journal of Experimental Psychology: Learning, Memory, and Cognition* 2013, Vol. 40, No. 4, 1142–1152.

6. K. A. Rose, I. G. Morgan, A. Kifley, S. Huynh, and W. Smith, "Outdoor Activity Reduces the Prevalence of Myopia in Children," *Ophthalmology*, 2008.

7. Q. Li, K. Morimoto, M. Kobayashi, H. Inagaki, M. Katsumata, Y. Hirata, K. Hirata, T. Shimizu, YJ Li, Y. Wakayama, T. Kawada, T. Ohira, N. Takayama, T. Kagawa, and Y. Miyazaki, "A Forest Bathing Trip Increases Human Natural Killer Activity and Expression of Anti-Cancer Proteins in Female Subjects," *International Journal of Immunopathology and Pharmacology*, 2007.

8. Peter James, Jaime E. Hart, Rachel F. Banay, and Francine Laden, "Exposure to Greenness and Mortality in a Nationwide Prospective Cohort Study of Women," *Environmental Health Perspectives*, 2016.

9. J. M. Jacobs, A. Cohen, R. Hammerman-Rozenberg, D. Azoulay, Y. Maaravi, and J. Stessman, "Going Outdoors Daily Predicts Long-Term Functional and Health Benefits among Ambulatory Older People," *Journal of Aging Research*, Volume 2013.

CHAPTER FIVE

1. Jolanda Maas, Robert A. Verheij, Peter P. Groenewegen, Sjerp de Vries, and Peter Spreeuwenberg, "Green Space, Urbanity, and Health: How Strong Is the Relation?" *Journal of Epidemiology and Community Health*, July 2006, Volume 60, Issue 7.

2. Lucy E. Keniger, Kevin J. Gaston, Katherine N. Irvine, and Richard A. Fuller, "What Are the Benefits of Interacting with Nature?" *Int J Environ Res Public Health*, 2013 Mar; 10(3): 913–935. Published online 2013 Mar 6. doi: 10.3390/ijerph10030913.

CHAPTER SIX

1. Gaétan Chevalier, PhD, Stephen T. Sinatra, MD, FACC, FACN, James Oschman, and Richard M. Delany, MD, FACC, "Earthing (Grounding) the Human Body Reduces Blood Viscosity: A Major Factor in Cardiovascular Disease," *Journal of Alternative and Complementary Medicine* 2013; 19(2): 102-110; published online at: http://online.liebertpub.com/doi/pdplus/10.1089/acm.2011.0820.

CHAPTER SEVEN

1. Jennie Rothenberg Gritz, "The Evolution of Alternative Medicine." *The Atlantic*, www.theatlantic.com/health/archive/2015/06/the-evolution-of-alternative-medicine/396458/.

CHAPTER EIGHT

1. E. R. Stothard, A. W. McHill, C. M. Depner, B. R. Birks, T. M. Moehlman, H. K. Ritchie, J. R. Guzzetti, E. D. Chinoy, M. K. LeBourgeois, J. Axelsson, and K. P. Wright Jr., "Circadian Entrainment to the Natural Light-Dark Cycle across Seasons and the Weekend." *Current Biology* 27: 1-6, 2017.

CHAPTER NINE

1. Thanai Pongdee, MD, FAAAAI, "Increasing Rates of Allergies and Asthma." American Academy of Allergy, Asthma & Immunology, www.aaaai.org/conditions-and-treatments/library/allergy-library/prevalence-of-allergies-and-asthma.

2. "Extreme Allergies and Global Warming." The National Wildlife Federation, www.nwf.org/~/media/PDFs/GlobalWarming/Reports/NWF_AllergiesFinal.ashx, 2010.

3. "Views of Allergy Specialists on the Health Effects of Climate Change," American Academy of Allergy, Asthma & Immunology, www.aaaai.org/Aaaai/media/MediaLibrary/PDF%20Documents/Libraries/Climate-Change-Survey.pdf December 2015.

4. Stephen T. Sinatra, MD, FACC, "New Hopes for Diabetes." The Earthing Institute, www.earthinginstitute.net/new-hope-for-diabetes.

5. Rob Rosedale, MD, "Cholesterol Is Not the Cause of Heart Disease." Mercola, Take Control of Your Health, https://articles.mercola.com/sites/articles/archive/2005/05/28/cholesterol-heart.aspx.

6. Gaétan Chevalier, PhD, Stephen T. Sinatra, MD, FACC, FACN, James Oschman, and Richard M. Delany, MD, FACC, "Earthing (Grounding) the Human Body Reduces Blood Viscosity: A Major Factor in Cardiovascular Disease." *Journal of Alternative and Complementary Medicine* 2013; 19(2): 102-110; published online at: http://online.liebertpub.com/doi/pdplus/10.1089/acm.2011.0820.

7. Institute of Medicine. "Sleep Disorders and Sleep Deprivation: An Unmet Public Health Problem." Washington, DC: The National Academies Press; 2006.

8. Andrew Weil, "Self Healing Sleep Deprivation." *Self Healing*. Date Unknown.

9. M. R. Irwin, R2. Olmstead, JE2 Carroll, "Sleep Disturbance, Sleep Duration, and Inflammation: A Systematic Review and Meta-Analysis of Cohort Studies and Experimental Sleep Deprivation." *Biological Psychiatry*, www.ncbi.nlm.nih.gov/pubmed/26140821, July 2016.

10. Geeta Ramesh, Peter J. Didier, John D. England, Lenay Santana-Gould, Lara A. Doyle-Meyers, Dale S. Martin, Mary B. Jacobs, and Mario T. Philipp. "Inflammation in the

Pathogenesis of Lyme Neuroborreliosis," (DOI: http://dx.doi.org/10.1016/j. ajpath.2015.01.024). This article appears online ahead of *American Journal of Pathology*, Volume 185, Issue 5 (May 2015) published by <u>Elsevier</u>.

11. Gaétan Chevalier, Stephen T. Sinatra, James L. Oschman, Karol Sokal, and Pawel Sokal, "Earthing: Health Implications of Reconnecting the Human Body to the Earth's Surface Electrons," *Journal of Environmental and Public Health*, Volume 2012 (2012), Article ID 291541, 8 pages.

12. Stephen T. Sinatra, "Grounding Helps Thin Dangerously Thick Blood and Fights Inflammation and Disease." Mercola.com, https://articles.mercola.com/sites/articles/archive/2013/08/04/barefoot-grounding-effect.aspx.

CHAPTER FOURTEEN

1. "2016 Yoga in America Study Conducted by Yoga Journal and Yoga Alliance Reveals Growth and Benefits of the Practice." *Yoga Alliance and Yoga Journal*, www.yogaalliance.org/Contact_Us/Media_Inquiries/2016_Yoga_in_America_Study_Conducted_by_Yoga_Journal_and_Yoga_Alliance_Reveals_Growth_and_Benefits_of_the_Practice.www.yogajournal.com/yogainamericastudy and www.yogaalliance.org/2016yogainamericastudy.

CHAPTER FIFTEEN

1. Alena Hall, "Meditation Is Even More Powerful Than We Originally Thought." www.huffingtonpost.com/2014/11/11/meditation-reduces-stress-harvard-study_n_6109404.html

CHAPTER SIXTEEN

1. Dr. Mark, "How to Lose Weight and Keep Your Dog Healthy by Walking." Pethelpful.com, https://pethelpful.com/dogs/lose-weight-walking-your-dog.

2. T. Galen Hieronymus, "Growing Plants in the Dark." *Journal of Borderland Research*, Vol. 44, No. 03. https://borderlandsciences.org/journal/vol/44/n03/Memoriam_to_T_Galen_Hieronymus.html.

3. Gary E. Schwartz, PhD, "Effects of Grounding Sunflowers." Grounded Beauty, https://groundedbeauty.com/case-studies/.

BIBLIOGRAPHY

Asprey, Dave. *The Bulletproof Diet*. New York: Rodale Books, 2014.

Asprey, Dave. *Headstrong: The Bulletproof Plan to Activate Untapped Brain Energy*. New York: Harper Wave, 2017.

Bowman, Katy. *Move Your DNA: Restore Your Health through Natural Movement*. Carlsborg, WA: Propriometrics Press, 2014.

Fenton, Mark, and Andrew Weil. *Walking: The Ultimate Exercise for Optimum Health*. Boulder, CO: Sounds True, 2006.

Gelb, Michael. *Body Learning: An Introduction to the Alexander Technique*. New York: Henry Holt, 1996.

Gelb, Michael. *How to Think Like Da Vinci: Seven Steps to Genius Every Day*. New York: Dell, Random House, Reissue 2000.

Gelb, Michael, and Kelly Howell. *Brain Power: Improve Your Mind as You Age*. Norato, CA: New World Library, 2012.

GROUNDED, Directed by Steve Kroschel, 2013. Haines, Alaska: One Paw Productions, A Steve Kroschel Film, DVD.

Hogan, Linda. *Walk Gently upon the Earth*. Lulu.com, 2009.

Howard, Brian Clark. "Connecting with Nature Boosts Creativity and Health." *National Geographic*, June 30, 2013.

Huffington, Arianna. *The Sleep Revolution: Transforming Your Life, One Night at a Time*. New York: Harmony, 2016.

Kamp, Jurriaan. *The Intelligent Optimist's Guide to Life: How to Find Health and Success in a World That's a Better Place Than You Think*. San Francisco, CA: Berrett-Koehler Publishers, 2014.

Louv, Richard. *Last Child in the Woods: Saving Our Children from Nature-Deficit Disorder*. New York: Algonquin Books, 2008.

Mehl-Medrona, Lewis. *Coyote Medicine, Lessons from Native American Healing*. New York: Simon & Schuster, 1997.

Mehl-Medrona, Lewis. *Coyote Healing: Miracles in Native Medicine*. Rochester, VT: Bear, 2003.

Mehl-Medrona, Lewis. *Coyote Wisdom: The Power of Story in Healing*. Rochester, VT: Bear, 2005.

Mercola, Joseph. *Effortless Healing*. New York: Harmony Books, 2015.

Nickel, Lori. "Aaron Rodgers Counting on Health Routine to Keep Him on Top for Years." *Milwaukee Wisconsin Journal Sentinel*, November 18, 2014.

Ober, Clinton, Stephen T. Sinatra, and Martin Zucker. *Earthing: The Most Important Discovery Ever!* Laguna Beach, CA: Basic Health Publications, 2014.

Selhub, Eve M., and Alan C. Logan. *Your Brain on Nature: The Science of Nature's Influence on Your Health, Happiness, and Vitality*. Toronto: Harper Collins, 2014.

Sinatra, Stephen T. *Revelations from Heaven and Earth*. New York: Rodale Books, 2015.

Snyder, Kimberly. *Radical Beauty: How to Transform Yourself from the Inside Out*. New York: Crown Publishing, Harmony, 2016.

Wachob, Jason. *Wellth: How I Learned to Build a Life, Not a Resume*. New York: Harmony, 2016.

Williams, Florence. *The Nature Fix*. New York: W. W. Norton, 2017.

INDEX

A ——————

Acupuncture, 19, 20, 51, 110, 111
Ailments, 13, 22, 33, 40, 60, 62, 78, 80, 105
Allergies, 62, 63, 68, 92
Ancestors, 22, 106
Animals, 6, 105, 106, 107
Anxiety, 19, 102, 103
Antioxidants, 15, 27, 74

Aristotle, 6, 32
Arteries, 48,66,67,87
Arthritis, 15, 33, 34, 40, 45, 46, 62, 64, 66
Asphalt 10, 28, 38, 76
Asprey, Dave, 98, 117
Asthma, 63
Athletes, 6, 10, 15, 46, 56, 57, 58

B ——————

Back Pain, 40, 59, 64, 97
Barefoot, 10, 13, 17, 19, 39, 45, 56, 58, 66, 71, 76, 81, 88, 91, 92, 102
Becker, Karen, 107
Blood, 16, 27, 35, 37, 38, 44, 47, 67, 87, 93, 110
    Pressure, 31, 35, 43, 47, 67, 93
    Viscosity, 33, 48, 67, 73, 93
Bowman, Katy, 43
Brooks, Judy, 6, 51, 52
Buddhists, 60, 103

C ——————

Cardiovascular, 48, 64, 67, 68, 69, 71, 96
Chevalier, Gaetan PhD, 6, 33, 48, 67
Chopra, Deepak, 51, 52
Circadian rhythms, 59, 98
Circulation, 16, 38, 52, 59, 87, 88, 89
Cement Sidewalks, 38
Concrete, 9, 10, 37, 38, 46, 76, 88
Crohn's Disease, 65
Currents, 25

Electric, 27
Cultures, 20, 22, 28, 109

D ——————

Depression, 16, 23, 31, 37, 79, 85, 97, 103
Diabetes, 22, 33, 43, 47, 63, 64, 65, 66, 67, 69, 71
Diet, 16, 17, 20, 27, 44, 51, 63, 65, 66, 68, 69, 81, 102, 107, 109
Diseases, 9, 15, 16, 20, 22, 27, 33, 34, 48, 62, 64, 65, 66, 71, 73, 74, 87, 92, 106, 110, 111
Dogs, 76, 106, 107

E ——————

Earth, 8, 10, 11, 13, 14, 19, 20, 22, 23, 25–29, 32, 33–35, 38, 39, 43, 44, 47, 54, 56, 58, 59, 60, 76, 78, 79, 84–85, 91–94, 97, 98, 101, 102, 103, 107, 110, 112
Earth Mothers, 91
Earthing Institute, 54
Electricity, 27, 78
Electrons, 8, 9, 14, 25–27, 38, 47, 56, 77, 78, 85, 88, 102
EMF, 29, 54, 78, 93
Energy, 8–10, 11, 14, 16, 19, 20, 22, 25–27, 33, 38–40, 51, 54, 56–58, 66, 69, 73, 74, 76, 80, 84–85, 92, 97, 100, 103, 109-111
Exercise, 20, 31, 39, 43, 64, 85

F ——————

Fatigue, 66
Feet, 14, 28, 38, 39, 45, 47, 50, 57, 58, 70, 76, 81, 85, 97, 102, 105, 111
Fenton, Mark, 43
Footwear, 9, 10, 28, 39, 56
Forest bathing, 37
Free Radicals, 9, 15, 26-27, 34, 47

G ——————

Garner, Christy, 101
Gelb, Michael, 6, 100

Gerson Institute, 44
Gerson, Max, 43
Grounded, 9, 11, 13–14, 20, 21, 27, 29, 34–35, 37, 41, 46, 47–48, 56–57, 59, 63, 65, 66, 71, 76, 80–82, 92-94, 101, 102, 105–107, 111, 112
Grounding, 1–11, 13–14, 34–35, 37-39, 43, 46–48, 50, 52, 56–58, 62, 73, 88, 92–94,

H ——————

Healing, 11, 13, 19–23, 28–29, 51–52, 79, 80, 84, 102, 109
Health, 11, 14, 16, 22, 26–29, 33–35, 54, 74, 80, 81, 82, 120
Heart, 20, 33, 47, 50, 65, 66–67, 72, 103
    Beats, 27
    Disease, 15, 33, 43, 47, 66–67
    Rate, 33
Hiking, 40, 82
Hippocrates, 20-21, 56, 59
Hogan, Linda, 6, 60
Howard, Brian Clark, 23
Huffington, Arianna, 67, 82
Hyman, Mark, 51

I ——————

Immunity, 16, 17, 37, 66, 68
Indigenous people, 11
Indoor, 77
    Grounding, 41
Inflammation, 15, 16, 64, 93
Inflammatory response, 47, 62
Insomnia, 34, 40, 67, 68, 69, 85

J ——————

Jain, Shamini, 6, 109–110
Jet lag, 38, 59, 98
Jobs, Steve, 32

K ——————

K1 point, 39
Kamp, Jurriaan, 6, 110
Kidney, 32, 39, 64, 70–71, 84

Koniver, Laura, 6, 38, 41, 60, 63, 80, 91
Kreek, Adam, 6, 56, 58, 81
Kroschel, Steve 6, 40, 41, 59, 105, 107

L ————————

Leather, 10, 13, 23, 28, 39, 44, 56
Leg, 31, 32, 66, 81, 85
Lifestyle, 11, 15, 16, 20, 22, 33, 47, 63, 65, 66, 74
Lightning, 26
Louv, Richard, 23, 37
Lyme Disease, 71

M ————————

Medications, 22, 45, 68, 70, 72, 93, 97
Medicine
    Energy medicine, 9, 52, 84
Meditation, 19, 20, 39, 40, 51, 58, 59, 66, 80, 85, 96, 102, 103, 109
Mehl-Madrona, Lewis, 6, 21–23, 59
    Coyote Healing, 21
    Coyote Medicine, 21
    Coyote Wisdom, 21
Melatonin, 35, 59
Mercola, Joseph, 43
Meridian Point, 19, 20, 39, 57
Mindfulness, 56, 81, 100, 101
Misconceptions, 50
Mitochrondria, 47, 56
Moccasins, 23, 28, 32, 39

N ————————

Native Americans, 6, 19, 21, 22, 23, 28, 32
Nature, 8, 10, 11, 14, 17, 19, 21, 22, 23, 28, 29, 31, 37–40, 50, 52, 57, 60, 70, 76, 80, 84, 94, 96, 97,101, 103, 105, 107, 109

O ————————

Ober, Clinton, 6, 8, 33, 34, 44, 46
Oschman, James, PhD, 6, 8, 9 33–34, 46, 50, 56, 67
Osteoporosis, 33, 46, 52, 71, 72
Oxygenation, 73

P ————————

Pain, 16, 22, 33, 34, 35, 40, 44, 45, 46, 48, 64, 65, 69, 84, 111
    Back, 40, 59, 64, 97
    Chronic, 9, 35, 52
    Joint, 70, 71
Pain reduction, 34
Pets, 66, 106, 107, 112
Pilates, 80
Plants, 40, 41, 79, 105, 107
Pluggz™, 88–89
Practitioners, 6, 10, 19, 20, 27, 34, 39, 51, 59, 81, 84, 96, 109, 112,

Q ————————

Qi, 19–20, 101
QiGong, 19–20, 100, 101

R ————————

Rest, 92
Running, 17, 58, 81, 92, 102

S ————————

Selhub, Eve, 37
Shoes, 10, 13, 28, 39, 44, 45, 54, 66, 76, 81, 88-89, 93, 111
Sinatra, Stephen, 6, 8, 33, 43, 48, 65, 67, 73, 74
Skeptics, 34, 50, 52, 54
Skin, 19, 23, 26, 27, 38, 39, 43, 52, 59, 65, 66, 71, 74, 78, 80, 87, 91
Sleep, 17, 33, 34–35, 46, 59, 67–70, 82, 92, 93
Snyder, Kimberly, 52, 66
Spencer, Jeff, 46
Sokal, Karol, 33, 34
Sokal, Pawel, 33, 34
Soles, 13, 14, 28, 39, 88,
Sports, 93, 101
Straus, Howard, 6, 43, 50
Stress, 15, 16, 31, 34, 35, 37, 46, 65, 66, 72, 103
Synthetic, 10, 28, 39, 50, 76, 111
Swimming, 43, 59, 64, 66, 103

T ————————

Tai Chi, 19, 20, 39, 80, 100, 102, 109
TED Talk, 103
Thundercloud, 26
Thyroid disease, 72
Training, Athletic, 58

Trees, 16, 22, 37, 40, 54, 59, 76, 97, 101, 103, 106

V ————————

Viscosity, 16, 33, 48, 67, 73, 93
Vitality, 37, 51, 84, 85
Vitamin D, 111
Voice America, 45

W ————————

Wachob, Jason, 102
Walking, 13, 14, 19, 20, 22, 31–32, 43, 58, 70, 102
Water, 14, 80, 103
    Conductivity of, 38
Weil, Andrew, 43, 81
Weintraub, Amy, 6, 97
Williams, Florence, 117

Y ————————

Yoga, 14, 17, 19, 39, 65, 72, 96–98, 103, 109
Youth, 17

Z ————————

Zucker, Martin, 8, 33